# What About ME?

## Seeing Yourself the Way God Sees You

### Vicki Courtney

PUBLISHING GROUP
Nashville, Tennessee

Published in association with the literary agency D.C. Jacobson & Associates, LLC, an Author Management Company, www.dcjacobson.com, and Alive Communications, Inc., an Author Management Company, www.alivecommunications.com.

978-1-4336-9176-8
Published by B&H Publishing Group
Nashville, Tennessee

Dewey Decimal Classification: J155.2
GIRLS \ SELF-ACCEPTANCE \ PERFECTIONISM (PERSONALITY TRAIT)

Printed in Huizhou, Guangdong, China, May 2016

1 2 3 4 5 6     20 19 18 17 16

You are absolutely beautiful.

-Song of Solomon 4:7

# Writer Bios

**Vicki Courtney** is a speaker and bestselling author of numerous books and Bible studies. She began writing about the culture's influence on tween and teen girls in 2003 and has a passion to see girls and women of all ages find their worth in Christ. Vicki is married to Keith, and they live in Austin, Texas. They are parents to three grown children, who are all married and live nearby. Vicki enjoys spending time at the lake, hanging out with her family, and spoiling her grandchildren rotten. More information about Vicki can be found at VickiCourtney.com.

**Ali Claxton** (Project Editor) is a freelance writer, editor, Bible study leader, mentor, storyteller, coffee drinker, aspiring novelist, and avid reader. She has a marketing degree and an MBA from Mississippi State University and is currently pursuing a master's degree in theological studies from the Southern Baptist Theological Seminary. She has served in girls' ministry for over a decade and loves seeing God move in the lives of teenagers.

**Pam Gibbs** is a writer, editor, speaker, youth minister, and amateur archer, but her favorite titles are wife and mom. She is a graduate of Southwestern Baptist Theological Seminary and leads teens at her church. When she's not hanging out with her tween daughter and teacher/coach husband, you'll find her curled up with a good mystery book and some dark chocolate.

**Tami Overhauser** is a blogger who writes about parenting, real life, and a really big God. She is a wife and busy mom to four children. Tami enjoys spending time with family (especially at the beach!), cooking, running, and laughing. More information about Tami can be found on her blog, RaisingAdam.com.

**Susan Palacio** has served professionally in ministry and missions for ten years, including a two-year stint serving in Guatemala. She is passionate about Truth and loves teaching women and girls. Susan and her husband, Carlos, live in Flower Mound, Texas, with their daughter, Emma, and are the owners of a coffeeshop (Trio Craft Coffee), which they opened for the purpose of "business as mission."

**Rachel Prochnow** is the founder of Radically Radiant Ministries, which is devoted to helping girls understand their immeasurable worth as daughters of the King. To learn more about Rachel and Radically Radiant Ministries, go to radicallyradiant.com.

**Meredith Derry** is originally from South Carolina and now resides in Nashville, Tennessee, with her husband, Alex. She is a marital and family therapist who loves to combine her passion for Scripture, her heart for families, and her love for writing in her everyday life.

**Kat Williamson** is a freelance writer and editor living in Dallas, Texas. She graduated from the University of Nebraska with a degree in communication studies and worked as an editor in the student ministry area of LifeWay Christian Resources for several years. She loves running, reading, and hanging out with her family.

**Whitney Prosperi** has a heart for girls and girls' ministry. She is the author of *Life Style: Real Perspectives from Radical Women in the Bible*, a twelve-week Bible study for middle and high school girls, as well as *Girls Ministry 101*, published by Youth Specialties. She lives in Tyler, Texas, with her husband, Randy, and daughters, Annabelle and Libby.

**Susie Davis** is the author of *Unafraid: Trusting God in an Unsafe World*. She and her husband, Will, cofounded Austin Christian Fellowship, where they pastor some of the most fabulous people in town. Susie loves McDonald's coffee, pink geraniums, and the yellow finches that flood her backyard every morning. For more info, visit her website: susiedavis.org.

# Introduction

I will never, ever forget the day I was voted the most popular girl in the sixth grade. I couldn't believe it. There were several other girls I thought for sure would be picked, but my classmates chose me! When I found out the results, my heart felt like it was going to jump right out of my chest and do a little dance right there in the middle of class.

After I was voted most popular, I got tons of calls to spend the night and invitations to birthday parties. I even got asked out by the most popular boy in class! Maybe that is when I became addicted to being popular. *Addicted* is a way of saying you are hooked on something—like you can't live without it. You might be addicted to chocolate or old *Full House* reruns. Or maybe you're addicted to Sonic crushed ice. (Guilty!) Some moms and girls are addicted to shopping. (Guilty again!)

My popularity addiction went on for years, and my life became all about doing whatever it took to stay in the popular group. Everything about my life looked normal on the outside, but on the inside I was worried about things like: *What if people stop liking me? What if I don't make cheerleader next year? What if the boys don't think I'm pretty? What if I'm not in the popular group next year . . . or the next . . . or the next?* And then my worst fear happened. I was never voted "most popular" again. In the years that followed, I was "sort of popular" but not the "most popular." When I lost the title, I lost some of my worth. The same thing happened when I didn't make the cheer squad one year . . . or win a ribbon in the track meet . . . or when I had an awkward growth spurt and didn't feel pretty.

You know how in math class you learned to do equations like this: $1 + 2 + 3 = 6$? In that equation, to get the answer 6, you have to add 1 and 2 and 3 together. Sometimes we can think of our worth, or what we feel about ourselves, like a math equation. We think we have to add together a bunch of things to feel good about ourselves. Let me show you what I mean.

## Pretty + Popular + Talented = Feeling good about myself

My heart felt happy when I was popular, people thought I was pretty, or I was good at something. Well, that's the problem with this math equation. If you take one or more of those things away (being pretty, being popular, being talented), it doesn't add up anymore, and you don't feel good about yourself. In fact, here is what my math equation looked like by the time I got to ninth grade:

## I have a big nose + I didn't get invited to Missy's party + I didn't make cheerleader = Feeling crummy about myself

Now that I'm older, I realize that my "worth equation" was all wrong. I shouldn't have based my worth (how I felt about myself) on being pretty, popular, or talented. Sure, we all want to be pretty, popular, and talented, but it becomes a problem when those things become so important that we can't feel good about ourselves when one or more of those things declines or goes away. Even if we have those things right now, it will change over the years and go up and down. But you know what never changes? How God thinks of us. Which is why we should base our worth on God's equation:

## Worth = What God thinks of me

It's time to think about yourself in a whole new way. I wrote *What About Me?* as a guide to help you see yourself through God's eyes rather than through the eyes of the world. You are priceless to God. You know how moms have tons of pictures of their kids on their phones? God loves you so much that if He had a wallet, your picture would be in it! Pretty amazing thought, huh? Who needs popularity when you can have that?!

Whether you read through this book on your own or grab a group of girls together and use it as a Bible study, my prayer is that by the time you turn the last page, you will base your worth on God's equation: Worth = What God thinks of you.

Your worth-crusader,

*Vicki Courtney*

# Contents

*P.S. As you read, you'll find several QR codes with questions next to them. Using any QR reader app, scan the codes to connect to some fun videos of girls giving their answers to the questions.*

When you see a QR code like this, scan it!

# MIRROR, MIRROR

# Pretty Packaging

## by Vicki Courtney

Have you ever been to one of those Christmas parties where everyone is told to bring either a joke gift or a fun gift, and then each person draws a number to see when they get to pick from the gift pile? I've been to many, but year after year, I make the same mistake. When it's my turn to pick a present, I always pick the one with the prettiest wrapping paper and matching bow. Because of the pretty packaging, I assume there must be an awesome gift inside. Like the year I unwrapped an awesome-looking gift and it was a not-so-awesome pair of furry kitty-cat earmuffs. Did I mention that I strongly dislike cats? Never mind that it doesn't even get cold enough where I live to wear earmuffs. Another time, I picked a present with oh-so-lovely wrapping, but inside was a not-so-lovely pair of used gym socks! Pretty on the outside doesn't always mean pretty on the inside.

Have you ever been lured by pretty packaging? Maybe you've been grocery shopping with your mom or dad and begged them for a product just because you liked the packaging. Product manufacturers who aim for successful sales know the importance of packaging. They know that customers can face thousands of items that bid for their attention, and their product better stand out if it's going to be noticed. Whether it's a pack of gum, a tube of toothpaste, or a bag of chips, you can bet that countless dollars and hours have been spent on researching which colors and designs will catch your eye. Product manufacturers want you to notice the product, and more importantly, to put it in your basket and scan it at the checkout. That's how they make money!

Now, what if I told you that you are also a product? Yes, you! If you are to catch the eye of the public, the packaging must be perfect. Or so the culture has told you. By the time you celebrate your twelfth birthday, you will have seen an estimated 77,546 commercials. Add to that number the images you see daily from magazines, billboards, and the Internet, and you will be bombarded with images of models and celebrities who look flawless. Perfect hair, perfect faces, and perfect bodies. Advertisers will use airbrushed models and celebrities to help

convince you that you can look just like them if you use the products they are selling. Only one problem—you're not airbrushed, so you will never look like them!

No wonder 93 percent of girls and young women report feeling anxiety or stress about some aspect of their looks when getting ready in the morning. That means if you have a group of a hundred girls, about ninety-three would say they feel stressed about their reflection in the mirror. More than half of girls (58 percent) describe themselves in negative terms, using words like *disgusting* and *ugly*, when feeling badly about themselves. Our culture today sends a message to women of all ages that beauty is about the packaging on the outside.

What would God have to say about *all* this? First Samuel says:

The LORD does not look at the things people look at. People look at the outward appearance, but the LORD looks at the heart. (16:7 NIV)

You are more than pretty packaging, so don't believe the culture's lie that you have to be flawlessly perfect on the outside. God is your maker, and He is more concerned with how pretty your heart is than your outer appearance.

The packaging doesn't matter—it's what's on the inside that really counts. Do you believe that?

## What About You?

1. Think about a time when you were drawn to pretty packaging. What was the item, and what about the packaging attracted your eye?

2. What sort of messages do girls get today about what they should look like on the outside?

3. What does God care more about: the outside or the inside?

What makes someone beautiful "on the inside"?

Scan for Video Answers!

# Pwiddy Gulls

### by Vicki Courtney

My daughter was one of those beautiful babies who got lots and lots of attention wherever she went. She was teeny-tiny for her age and had beautiful fair skin, blonde curly hair, blue eyes, and a sparkling personality. When she started walking, people often commented that she looked like a walking baby doll. In the beginning, I loved the attention she got and would smile proudly when people commented on how adorably cute she was.

Of course, she was just a baby and didn't realize why she was getting the attention—until one day when she was about three years old. I remember we were walking along a sidewalk and she caught a glimpse of her reflection in a shop window and said, "Ooh, pwiddy gull." At the time, I thought it was perfectly adorable and thought to myself, *Wow, this kid is going to grow up and feel really good about herself!*

About a year later, however, I realized we had a problem. She was four years old and in preschool. It was picture day at her school, and we put on her prettiest dress with the matching hair ribbon. When I dropped her off at the door that morning, her teacher said, "Paige, you are such a pretty girl." And instead of saying thank you, my child brushed by her teacher with a sideways glance and said, "I know. Everyone tells me that." I was so embarrassed! After that, I quit making comments about her outer beauty and tried to compliment her more on her inner beauty. I would say things like, "Paige, you are so kind to let your friend have the cupcake with the most icing," or, "Paige, you are sweet to read your little brother a book." I didn't want her to grow up thinking that she was only special if she was a "pwiddy gull." Besides, everyone knows that "pwiddy little gulls" don't always grow up to be "pwiddy *big* girls," right?

The Bible says that "beauty does not last" (Proverbs 31:30 NLT). I'm sure you've noticed by now that as people get older, their bodies start to *look* older. That's why I feel sorry for really pretty people who only feel good about themselves because they are pretty. Someday they will look in the mirror and see wrinkles on their foreheads and around their eyes, and they will notice that their hair is getting gray. If they haven't learned that beauty really comes from the inside, they will look in the mirror and not like the person staring back at them.

Today my daughter is all grown-up, and she is still a very "pwiddy gull." Most importantly, she is "pwiddy" on the inside. My daughter knows that when God looks at her, He doesn't look at her outer appearance—He looks at her heart. She knows that the best beauty secret is to see herself through God's eyes. Remember the Bible verse that talked about beauty not lasting? Well, the last part of that verse has the best beauty secret ever. Do you want to be "greatly praised" for your inner beauty? Then fear the Lord! That doesn't mean that you are supposed to be afraid of God. It's talking about a different kind of fear. It means to think and speak highly of God. Don't use bad words or say the Lord's name in vain (saying curse words with "God" or "Jesus" in them). Give God the attention He deserves. Talk to Him daily. Thank Him for all He has done for you. Read your Bible so you can learn more about Him. That's what it means to "fear the Lord."

There will be some very beautiful people who get to heaven and discover that their outer beauty means nothing to God. He will not be impressed. There is only one thing God is interested in: our hearts. What do you look like on the inside?

So, have you discovered the best beauty secret ever? Do you fear the Lord? Well, keep it up, and someday you just might stand before God and hear Him say, "Pwiddy gull!"

## What About You?

1. Do you feel good about who you are? Why or why not?

2. Do you spend a lot of time thinking about what you look like?

3. Why is it more important for you to be beautiful on the inside than on the outside?

# QUIZ

## Would You Rather . . .

Circle your choices below:

Hang out in a big group of friends or with one friend?

Go to the mall or a bookstore?

Wear pants or a skirt?

Eat fast food or fancy food?

Be smart or athletic?

Go to the beach or mountains on vacation?

Own a cat or a dog?

Wear your hair down or in a ponytail?

Water-ski or snow-ski?

Eat salty or <u>sweet</u> foods?

Ride a roller coaster or a <u>Ferris wheel</u>?

<u>Watch TV</u> or read a book?

<u>Eat cake</u> or pie for dessert?

Take dance class or <u>art class</u>?

Live in a <u>big city</u> or a small town?

Listen to <u>pop</u> or country?

Sleep with a <u>night-light</u> or in the pitch dark?

Wear <u>socks</u> or have bare feet?

Play board games or <u>computer games</u>?

# Dare to Be You

## by Vicki Courtney

I love shopping. For as long as I can remember, I've loved getting new clothes and shoes. Who doesn't love the feeling of looking in the mirror and thinking, *Wow, I look good. Really good!*? And that's exactly how I felt when my mom took me shopping in the sixth grade for a new outfit to wear to a special occasion. I can't remember the special occasion, but I sure can remember that outfit. I couldn't wait to show it to my friends.

The following week, a couple of my friends came over after school, and I told them about my new outfit. Of course, they wanted to see it, so I slipped into my closet to put it on while they waited outside the door. When I came out, they oohed and aahed, and I felt good that they approved of my outfit. Until, that is, I went back into my closet to change. The door was cracked, and I happened to look out just in time to see one of my friends grimacing and shaking her head to my other friend, as she silently mouthed, "I don't like it." Ouch, that hurt!

I'm ashamed to say I never wore that outfit again after the special occasion, and I'm sure I was self-conscious the whole time I wore it. It got the thumbs-down from one friend, and all of a sudden, that outfit turned *I look good* into *I look stupid.* I allowed one friend to dictate what I saw in the mirror and, more importantly, how I felt about myself.

Even though that moment happened nearly forty years ago, I still remember it in detail. Isn't that crazy? It shows just how much I based my worth on the opinions of others. Sure, we all like approval, but when we reach a point where we change our tastes and opinions to earn the approval of others, we lose ourselves.

If I could go back and do it all over again, I would have listened to a different voice in that closet when I saw my friend grimace and say she didn't like my outfit. I would have shrugged it off and said (not out loud, of course!), *Vicki, you LOVE this outfit, and that's all that matters. It's okay to have a different style sense than your friends. If you like your reflection, wear it! Be who you are instead of who others want you to be.*

Is it hard for you to be . . . YOU?

Do you believe you are "remarkably and wonderfully made" (Psalm 139:14)?

Girls who look to God to define their worth don't worry about fitting into the world's mold. They know they are unique and like no one else, so they don't bother with trying to be someone they're not. They are comfortable with the person they are.

There's a quote I love that says, "Be yourself. Everyone else is taken." I like that quote because it's a reminder that God made us all different for a reason. How boring would the world be if we all looked the same way and shared all the same likes and dislikes?

The next time you find yourself in a situation where you are tempted to be someone you're not, remember that you are "remarkably and wonderfully made." Dare to be the "you" God created you to be. Dare to be YOU.

## What About You?

1. Is it hard for you to be you?

2. Can you think of a time when you changed your mind about something because you wanted to fit in but it wasn't really who you are? Describe what happened.

3. Look up Psalm 139:14 and write it out below. Try to memorize the verse and quote it when you are tempted to fit in and not be your true self.

# 10 Super Cool Things About You

1. You have 60,000 miles of blood vessels cruising through your body (more than twice the distance around the earth).

2. Your heart beats more than 100,000 times a day.

3. You have around 650 muscles with at least 6,000,000,000 muscle fibers in each.

4. While you read this sentence, 50 million cells in your body will die and be replaced.

5. You produce 4 cups of saliva every day.

6. A sneeze zooms out of your mouth at more than 100 miles per hour.

7. You spent about one to two hours as a single cell.

8. Your brain generates more electrical impulses in a day than all the telephones in the world put together.

9. Your eye can distinguish 500 shades of gray.

10. You have approximately 100,000 hairs on your head.

# Beauty by the Book

## by Vicki Courtney

**Psalm 139:14 NIV**
I praise you because I am fearfully and wonderfully made; your works are wonderful, I know that full well.

**What it means:** You are created in the image of God, and God doesn't make junk! Every person is unique and different, like a snowflake. No two are the same. God sees you as a masterpiece, and when you look in the mirror, He wants you to "know that full well." Try this beauty tip: every morning when you look in the mirror, say Psalm 139:14 and smile. You might even tape the verse up on your mirror as a reminder!

**1 Samuel 16:7**
But the LORD said to Samuel, "Do not look at his appearance or his stature, because I have rejected him. Man does not see what the LORD sees, for man sees what is visible, but the LORD sees the heart."

**What it means:** The world focuses on what people look like on the outside. God focuses on what people look like on the inside. Do you put more time and effort into being pretty on the outside or the inside? As you get older, you will meet Christian girls who spend more time trying to find the perfect outfit, get the perfect tan, find the perfect lip gloss, and have the perfect body. Although there's nothing wrong with wanting to look pretty, we need to make sure it's in balance. God would rather see us work on becoming drop-dead gorgeous on the inside. You know, the kind of girl who talks to Him on a regular basis in prayer and reads her Bible.

## Proverbs 31:30
Charm is deceptive and beauty is fleeting, but a woman who fears the LORD will be praised.

**What it means:** Beauty fades with age, so if you are more concerned with your outer appearance, you will be unhappy when the wrinkles come and the number on the scale goes up. A sign of beauty is "fearing" the Lord. That doesn't mean to be afraid of God, but rather to be amazed at Him and all He has done. To "fear God" is to love and respect God.

## 1 Peter 3:3–4
Your beauty should not consist of outward things like elaborate hairstyles and the wearing of gold ornaments or fine clothes. Instead, it should consist of what is inside the heart with the imperishable quality of a gentle and quiet spirit, which is very valuable in God's eyes.

**What it means:** This does not mean it's wrong to braid your hair or wear nice clothes and jewelry. The verse was written to warn women not to follow the customs of some of the Egyptian women who, during that time period, spent hours and hours working on their hair, makeup, and outfits. God would rather see women working on becoming beautiful on the inside—the kind of beauty that lasts forever.

## 1 Timothy 4:8 NLT
Physical training is good, but training for godliness is much better, promising benefits in this life and in the life to come.

**What it means:** Exercising and staying in shape is a good thing, but God expects us to stay in shape spiritually by reading our Bibles, praying, and going to church on a regular basis. In other words, there will be plenty of people who put their time and effort into staying in shape, but they could be out of shape spiritually. If they don't know Jesus Christ, their perfect bodies won't get them through the gates of heaven.

# Beautiful Role Models

## by Ali Claxton

A role model is someone we look up to, someone who sets an example we can follow, or someone who teaches us a lesson we need to learn as we grow. No one can be a perfect role model (except Jesus), but we find some incredible women in Scripture who show us what true beauty looks like. Find the names of the women described below by looking up the verses listed. Write each name (or description) in the blank as you go.

_____ She found favor with God (Luke 1:30-31).

_____ She won a beauty contest, became queen, and used her position for God's glory (Esther 2:17; 4:14).

_____ She loved sitting at the feet of Jesus and listening to Him (Luke 10:38-42).

_____ She gave everything she had to God (Mark 12:41-44).

_____ She opened her home to bless others (Acts 16:14-15).

_____ She followed God's plan for her life (Ruth 1:16).

_____ She offered the Lord what was most precious to her (1 Samuel 1:22-28).

_____ She loved to help others (Acts 9:36).

These women lived many years ago, but the examples they set make them great role models for us today. They teach us what it means to be beautiful from the inside out. See, that's the thing about beauty—it starts on the inside of a person and works its way out. Women who love the Lord and are living for His glory radiate with a lasting beauty that never fades!

## What About You?

1. Who are the role models you look up to right now?

2. Why do you want to be like them?

3. Are you a good role model for others? Can people tell that you love God based on your actions and attitudes?

# If I Could Change One Thing . . .

## by Vicki Courtney

We surveyed girls your age and asked them what was one thing they would change about themselves, if it were possible. Interestingly, most girls said they would change nothing, which is awesome! That means many girls your age are comfortable with the person God created them to be. Of course, that doesn't mean that we don't struggle from time to time, wishing we could change something about our appearance or our character.

One thing I noticed about the survey answers was that most girls who wanted to change something mentioned something related to their appearance. That tells me many girls feel pressured to look a certain way, and it's important for each of you to know that you are beautiful just the way you are.

### What about you? What would you change?

Nothing: I like myself the way I am. I like how God made me.

| | |
|---|---|
| Zahara, 11 | Emily, 10 |
| Gia, 9 | Laura, 10 |
| Claire, 10 | Jordyn, 9 |
| Elizabeth, 10 | Lisa, 8 |
| Sydney, 10 | Kimberley, 11 |
| Molly, 11 | Meagan, 10 |
| Mara, 10 | Morgan, 11 |
| April, 11 | Caroline, 9 |
| Madeleine, 10 | Kelsey, 12 |
| Elise, 10 | Taylor, 11 |
| Lauren, 10 | Angela, 12 |
| Stephanie, 11 | Riley, 11 |
| | Joclyn, 11 |

To be skinnier.
   Anne, 11

To be taller.
   Grace, 9

I'd be better at math.
   Theresa, 12

I would have no braces.
   Savannah, 12

My habit of biting my nails.
   Kayla, 10

I would be outgoing.
   Danielle, 11

Being able to speak up about my feelings.
   Kristie, 11

Change my hair color to reddish-orange
because my best friend has that color.
   Kristin, 12

That I could control my anger better.
   Emily, 10

My body.
   Chloe, 9

How I act at school.
   Taylor, 11

My attitude.
   Casie, 10

My teeth.
    Valerie, 9    Kaleigh, 10
    Marissa, 10  Gretchen, 11

That I didn't have allergies.
    Jessica, 8

Height.
    Julie, 11

Not to be allergic to food.
    Jaimee, 10

To be older.
    Olivia, 9

That I didn't have dry skin.
    Bethany, 12

To be more trustworthy.
    Kaelan, 10

No freckles.
    Ellie, 9

That I would learn to dance.
    Breanna, 12

That I worship God more.
    Morgan, 10

To be a better friend.
    Grace, 8

My glasses. They itch me.
    Stephanie, 10

My legs.
    Lara, 11    Andie, 12

To be a faster runner.
    Amy, 12

To be left-handed instead of right-handed.
    Morgan, 11

I wish I didn't have warts.
    Emily, 12

The way my voice sounds (I have a deep voice, and I don't like it).
    Brooke, 11

To have perfect vision.
    Saige, 10

My weight.
    Angela, 8

Freckles on the face.
    Brittani, 11

My height.
    Nicole, 9

My attitude.
    Amber, 9

My hair.
    Alex, 10
    Karly, 9
    Rachel, 10
    Mikaela, 10
    Merissa, 10

Hair color.
    Allison, 10
    Samantha, 10
    Allison, 8

My hair because I want it to
be straight and more blonde.
    Kennan, 8

My name.
    Danielle, 9

I would be more loving to my sisters.
    Alyssa, 8

I would not need glasses. But I
    know that God made me just
    right.
    Ellie, 11

I wish I was more outgoing.
    Sarah Grace, 10

I would be REALLY popular at school.
    Heather, 9

My personality.
    AnnaLee, 10

My tummy. It kind of sticks out.
    Melissa, 9

I would like not to be dyslexic so
school would be easier.
    Melissa, 11

My eye color.
   Faith, 11

The size of my feet.
   Jenica, 11

My tendency to fear the future instead of think about the great things God is doing now.
   Mayson, 11

My voice. I have a really low voice, and I wish it would be a little higher.
   Karon, 11

To make my zits go away forever.
   Emma, 9

I wouldn't be so hard on myself. I know it's good to push yourself, but you shouldn't be too tough on yourself when you fall a little short of your expectations.
   Courtney, 11

I would want to be taller because I am small. People call me shrimp!
   Breeann, 11

That I could run faster.
   Rachel, 11

# If the Shoe Fits

## by Vicki Courtney

I remember it like it was yesterday. It was fitting day for my new eighth-grade cheerleading uniform, and the entire cheer squad was gathered together in a small fitting room with our coach. I had looked forward to this day since making the squad. Sample tops, sweaters, and pleated skirts were strewn about the room. The goal was to try them on and find your size. Last on the list were the shoes. I was probably more excited about the shoes than anything else because I've loved shoes for as long as I can remember. It might have something to do with the fact that my grandfather owned a shoe store. I have fond memories of visiting his store as a little girl and trying on shoe after shoe in his stockroom. And of course, he usually let me pick out a pair to take home when I was old enough to finally fit in the smallest size he offered in his store—a 5 1/2. I always wanted to have a petite foot, but as luck would have it, my feet grew faster than any other part of my body. By the time I was a middle schooler, I wore a size 8 shoe, which on my petite frame made me feel like I had giant clown feet.

Honestly, I didn't think much about it until I was trying on cheer shoes with the other girls my age in the fitting room. Most of them were ordering sizes 5 or 6, and a couple of them ordered a size 7. And then it was my turn to try on the sample shoes. I slipped on the size 7 and boy, was it ever tight! One of my friends asked, "Does it fit?" and before I knew it, I answered, "Yes, it fits perfectly!" The uniform consultant wrote size 7 next to my name and told our group she had everything she needed to place the order for our uniforms.

When my uniform and shoes arrived, I could hardly wait to try everything on. The pleated skirt and tops fit perfectly! But the shoes . . . yeah, about that. My size 8 feet wanted nothing to do with the size 7 shoes I ordered. I tried to walk around in them and attempted to convince myself that it wasn't a big deal for my toes to be scrunched up, forcing me to waddle around like a wounded duck. The first football game was in a couple of weeks, and the cheerleaders always wore their uniforms to school on games days. I knew there was no way I would be able to survive an entire day in the one-size-too-small shoes, so I told my mom I had ordered the wrong size.

Fortunately, when she contacted the uniform company, they agreed to swap the shoes out for the right size, and I got them just in time for the first game.

So, why am I telling you this story? As you move through your tween years, a lot of changes are taking place in your bodies. Some of you will grow taller than most of the other girls your age, and you will wish you weren't so tall. Others of you will be the shortest girls in your grade, and you will wish you weren't so short. Some of you will develop faster and may need a bra sooner than your friends. You might be embarrassed by the changes taking place. And then there are girls who will develop very slowly and wish they could wear a bra like some of their friends. Maybe you have curly hair and wish it was straight. Or maybe you have straight hair and wish it was curly. Or maybe you wear a size 8 (or larger) shoe and wish your feet were smaller, like I did.

Here's the deal. If I could go back and have a little chat with my eighth-grade self before that uniform fitting, I'd tell her, "Look, girl, if the shoe fits, wear it!" In other words, own your differences rather than wishing you were just like everyone else. Every girl is struggling with something about her body that is different.

Curly hair? Own it.

Straight hair? Own it.

Big-boned? Own it.

Small-boned? Own it.

Tall? Own it.

Short? Own it.

Freckles? Own it.

Ears that stick out? Own it.

Face breaking out? Own it.

Big feet? Own it.

Small feet? Own it.

Red hair? Own it.

Birthmark? Own it.

Outie belly button? Own it.

I have an idea. Every time you find yourself frustrated over the things about you that are different, stop and say a silent prayer to God. Thank Him for making you different and special.

Are you ready to own it when it comes to the things that make you different?

If the shoe fits, wear it!

## What About You?

1. Can you think of a time when a difference in your appearance or body development made you wish you were like everyone else?

2. Below, write down your differences, and beside each one, write, "I own it." Now say a short prayer and thank God for making you different.

# Body Development

## What's Your One Worry?

### by Vicki Courtney

When we surveyed girls your age, we asked them if they had any worries about body development. Most girls were worried about starting their period—which, by the way, is completely normal! In fact, all the answers we got are completely normal things that many girls worry about.

The important thing to remember is that God has "fearfully and wonderfully" made you (Psalm 139:14 NIV). Take peace in knowing that you will develop at the pace He has determined, and you will have the exact body shape that He intended. Body shape is different from weight. God wants you to be healthy and eat right, especially during this important time in your life when your body is developing. That means being in a weight range that is healthy for you. In the meantime, no worries! He has everything under control!

# When it comes to body development, what is one thing you're kinda-sorta worried about?

- Starting my period.—Savannah, 12; Kayla, 10; Danielle, 11; Kelly, 12; Alex, 10; Karly, 9; Chloe, 9; Jaimee, 10; Jessica, 9; Elise, 10; Allison, 10; Riley, 10

- My period might start at school.—Corrie, 11

- That when my chest develops, it will draw attention.—Taylor, 11

- Getting fat.—Casie, 10; Emily, 10

- Being the last one to develop.—Elise, 12

- Boys staring at me when I start developing.—Rachel, 10

- Not being physically strong. I'm really skinny, and I'm not curvy!—Bethany, 12

- Not being tall.—Kaelan, 10

- That I won't develop in certain places.—Breanna, 12

- Not being tall enough.—Sarah, 10

- Getting fat. I always want to stay fit—it really worries me. —Keagan, 10

- That I'll be too tall and clumsy.—Morgan, 11

- That people will look at me differently because I'm maturing faster than my friends.—Emily, 12

# Thanking God for Your Bod

## by Vicki Courtney

*H*ave you ever stood in front of your mirror and huffed under your breath, "I don't like my body"? Have you ever wished you had longer legs, straighter hair, or stronger muscles for sports? Or maybe you've wished you didn't have freckles, fair skin, or that weird birthmark. Do you dream of being heavier, thinner, taller, or shorter? If you have answered yes to any of these, you are not alone. We can all fall into the "I wish" trap. You know what I'm talking about. *I wish I was as skinny as so-and-so. I wish I was as pretty as she is. I wish my nose wasn't so big. I wish my ears didn't stick out so much. I wish, I wish, I wish.* You get the picture.

What causes the "I wish" trap? Sometimes we compare ourselves to other people. The crazy thing is, those "other people" are probably also comparing themselves to other people! Or maybe you compare yourself to girls you see on television or in magazines who look perfect. You know the ones I'm talking about. They have perfect hair that is never messed up. They have perfect skin and perfect legs and perfect everything. Well, let me tell you a little secret about that. They are really not as perfect as they look. For one thing, they are wearing a lot of makeup, and they had it put on by a professional makeup artist who knows how to make it look perfect. Most of the models in the magazines have had their pictures "touched up." What that means is that someone has used a computer to make that model look perfect. Airbrushing can take away freckles or make a model's legs look skinnier. You can even change a model's hair color or the color of the shirt she is wearing in the picture. If you wanted to, you could add silly Mickey Mouse ears on her head and give her a mustache. In real life, she looks more like you and me.

I wish I had known that when I was your age. I always compared myself to other people, and I had a hard time accepting the body God gave me. I fell into the "I wish" trap. I wanted to look in the mirror and like what I saw, but I couldn't because I was always wishing for something else. Today, many years later, I like my reflection in the mirror. So, what's my secret? I realized that God doesn't make junk and that every time I wished for this or that, I was basically telling God that I wasn't happy with the body He gave me.

Of course, I'm not saying that it's okay to eat five bags of Oreos and become a lazy couch potato. I'm talking about accepting your body shape for what it is: short, tall, big-boned, or petite. The true test is to be able to look at yourself in the mirror and confidently say, "I praise you because I am fearfully and wonderfully made; your works are wonderful, I know that full well" (Psalm 139:14 NIV). If you can't say it and mean it, consider putting the verse on your mirror as a reminder and saying it every day. Pray and ask God to help you believe it. God knew exactly what He was doing when He created you.

## What About You?

1. Are you happy with the body shape God gave you? Why or why not?

2. Do you believe you are "fearfully and wonderfully made" by the Creator of the universe?

3. Are you taking care of the body God has given you? Why or why not?

# What Makes a Girl?
## by Susie Davis

You are a girl whether or not you like pink! Being a girl is not just about what kind of clothes you wear or what you like to do on the weekends. It's not just about whether you want to paint your toenails or wear lip gloss. Girls are all different. Just look around you. Some girls like to watch football with their dads, and some girls like to go shopping with their moms—but no matter what, they are all girls just the same.

The fact is, being a girl is something God designed you to be when He created you. Psalm 139:13 says, "For you created my inmost being; you knit me together in my mother's womb" (NIV). God made you a girl in your mother's womb. There was nothing that you did or didn't do to be created that way. God decided. And that's why in the hospital when you were born, the first thing the doctor said to your parents was, "It's a GIRL!" A wonderful girl!

# Perfectly Imperfect

## by Vicki Courtney

No one saw my daughter's secret tears over a flaw she has struggled with since she was a small child. No one knew the anxiety that sparked in her heart over simple things most people don't think twice about. Like when a group circles up to pray and someone suggests that everyone hold hands. Or that time I signed her up for cotillion—a ballroom dance class for boys and girls—when she was in sixth grade. Or when she became a flier on her competitive cheer team in middle school. Or when she had her first boyfriend in high school and knew it was only a matter of time before he would find out. No one knew her secret, until they held her hand.

You see, when my daughter is nervous, her hands sweat. Oh sure, that happens to a lot of people, but her hands sweat a lot. In fact, they sweat even when she's not nervous. She has a condition called hyperhidrosis, and it made her life difficult during her preteen and teen years. Sometimes she even thought about not doing certain things she enjoyed just so she could keep her imperfection a secret. As she got older, it didn't bother her as much, and she began to accept her condition.

Everyone has imperfections or weaknesses that can make life difficult. In the Bible, the apostle Paul spoke of a "thorn in the flesh" (2 Corinthians 12:7) but never revealed what the "thorn" was. He wasn't complaining about a real, actual thorn in his flesh (ouch!), but rather an imperfection. How did he feel about this thorn? Take a look:

> Three different times I begged the Lord to take it away. Each time he said, "My grace is all you need. My power works best in weakness." So now I am glad to boast about my weaknesses, so that the power of Christ can work through me. That's why I take pleasure in my weaknesses, and in the insults, hardships, persecutions, and troubles that I suffer for Christ. For when I am weak, then I am strong. (2 Corinthians 12:8–10 NLT)

If God had wanted us to know what Paul's thorn in the flesh was, He would have told us. It's as simple as that. But He didn't. I believe God didn't include this information because everyone has a thorn in the flesh—a flaw, an imperfection, or something that can cause grief and sadness in life—and no matter what it is, we should have the same attitude about it that Paul did. My daughter's thorn was her sweaty hands. Someone else's thorn may be a birth defect or a learning disability. Others may struggle with anxiety or depression. Others may struggle with being overweight or underweight. If it's a struggle and it causes you grief, it is a thorn.

## What is your thorn in the flesh?

Let me ask you this. Can you boast (brag) about it? No, probably not! That's a hard thing to do. The point Paul was trying to make was that our struggles and imperfections make us feel weak; and when we feel weak, we depend on Christ's strength to get us through it. Did you know your imperfections can actually make you stronger if you give them over to Christ? That doesn't mean He'll take them away—remember, He didn't take Paul's thorn away. But it does mean He'll give us the strength we need to deal with the thorn, and it will draw us closer to Christ in the process.

When you understand the reason for your imperfections, you will be able to "boast" about them. What that verse really means is that we should be willing to talk about our weaknesses and boast or brag about the strength Christ gives us to deal with them.

For example, maybe your thorn is that you are dyslexic and you have a hard time reading because you see the letters in the wrong order. You hate your thorn in the flesh because it makes you feel weak. You've even cried about it to your parents. Your biggest fear is that you'll be asked to read out loud. You're afraid because it takes you longer to process the words on the page, so you read slower than your peers. Maybe your Sunday school teacher doesn't know about your dyslexia, and one Sunday, she asks you to read a verse from the Bible out loud. You immediately get that hot feeling all over, and you worry about what your friends in class will think when they hear you reading. What would you do?

Instead of stressing out about it, what if you were just honest with your group? What if before you read aloud, you said something like, "Okay, before I read the verse, I need you to know I have this thing called dyslexia, and it takes me a little bit longer to read words on a page. It's something I've prayed about, but I'm thankful for it because it makes me look to God for strength." By sharing it with others, you no longer allow it to make you feel "less than," but rather, you point out to the group how Christ makes you feel "more than." It also gives others in your group the courage to share their own imperfections. And for the record, anyone who makes fun of you—especially after you have been honest about your thorn—is not a friend worth having. They have bigger problems than dyslexia, and they need your prayers.

The next time you are sad and worried about an imperfection, think about Paul's thorn in the flesh and the remedy he gave us to overcome our imperfections. God's power works best in weakness. Do you believe that?

## What About You?

1. What is your "thorn in the flesh"? (It's okay to list more than one!)

2. How has this "thorn" or imperfection caused you sadness or grief?

3. Do you think it's possible to thank God for your imperfections?

4. What might you say to others that will point to Christ's strength rather than your weakness? Write out what you plan to say below.

# True Reflections

## by Vicki Courtney

Years ago, one of my aunts gave me a beautiful old fabric purse that had been in the family for many years. I tucked it away in a drawer for safekeeping, and I recently stumbled upon it. I wondered how old the purse might be, so I pulled it out to take a closer look. To my surprise, I found a type-written note inside that hinted at its age. The note began with a brief timeline of ownership: "This purse belonged to Byrd Siglar Carey, mother of . . . " and so on through the family tree, right down to my aunt's husband. I'm assuming my uncle typed the note, as he was the last person listed in the handy timeline. He ended the note with: "The purse is now (1977) about ninety years old."

So, I had my answer. The purse dates back to the 1880s or 1890s. In addition to the coolness factor of the name Byrd, (maybe her nickname was Birdie?), there were a couple of other treasures tucked inside her purse: a tiny hand-stitched satin coin purse and a small compact mirror. While finding a compact mirror in a woman's purse today would not be a big deal, it was very special to have one in the late 1800s. In fact, it wasn't until the early 1900s that mirrors began to appear in homes over the bathroom sink. For that reason, girls didn't grow up seeing their reflection often. They might catch it here and there when they walked by a pond and saw their reflection in the water or by a store window and caught a glimpse of themselves in the glass.

It's weird to think about a time when mirrors weren't a part of everyday life. How did girls get ready for school in the mornings? How did they check to see if food was stuck in their teeth? Did everyone have messy, unkempt hair? As strange as it seems, girls back then didn't have the same pressures girls today have because they didn't grow up studying their reflections in a mirror and comparing what they saw to other young women.

I am certainly not saying it's wrong to have mirrors. (I have lots of them!) The important thing is to know your true reflection in the eyes of God. Genesis 1:27 says, "So God created man in His own image; He created him in the image of God." What the verse means is that God created each of us to look like Him! That doesn't mean God looks like a person.

It means we can think about things, choose things, and understand right and wrong. And that means we can honor Him through patience, loving-kindness, honesty, selflessness, and so on. That is the "reflection" that matters most to God.

What do you see when you look in the mirror?

What is your favorite thing about the way you look?

Scan for Video Answers!

## What About You?

1. Imagine for a minute how things might be different if you and all your friends grew up without mirrors. How might that change how girls feel about themselves?

2. Are you more worried about having a pretty face or a pretty heart?

3. What runs through your head when you see your reflection in the mirror? Do you like what you see, or do you wish you could change your reflection?

4. Write down below what you think it means to be "made in the image of God."

# Quick Beauty Tips

## by Vicki Courtney

*Y*ou've probably heard your mom say that "beauty comes from the inside" and thought, *Yeah, right, Mom—tell other people that*. Well, believe it or not, your mom is right. So what really makes a girl beautiful? Try these beauty secrets:

**Smile:** If you haven't discovered this "free face-lift," try smiling more often. It will brighten your entire face.

**Voice:** Does your voice sound confident and mature? Some girls carry their "baby talk" voice into their young adult years, and it is not attractive. If you sound like a baby when you talk, chances are, you will be treated like a baby. Let's leave the baby talk for the real babies!

**Eye contact:** As you speak with people, look into their eyes. When you nervously dart your eyes back and forth, it makes you look shy and insecure.

**Posture:** When I was your age, my mother used to constantly tell me to quit slumping my shoulders and to stand up straight. It drove me crazy . . . until I saw a picture of myself one day and was horrified! My posture made me look so insecure that I made a concentrated effort to pull my shoulders back and stand taller.

**Outward focus:** If a friend has shared a difficulty with you or has expressed sadness over something, do you remember to ask her how she is doing the next time you see her? You can even write her a note, send her a text, or call her to see how she is doing.

**Humor:** Have you learned to laugh at yourself when you do something embarrassing? Each one of us is going to blow it from time to time, whether we trip and fall or say something that doesn't make sense. Rather than act uncomfortable, just crack up! If you don't make a big deal of it, chances are, no one else will either.

**Admitting weaknesses:** Everyone has weaknesses—it's a fact. Don't feel that you always have to pretend to have your act together. If you make a mistake, just own it and say, "Whoops, I made a mistake." You won't believe how good it feels!

**Rejoicing with others:** Very few people (including Christians) can really be happy when others around them succeed at something or have something wonderful happen to them. However, the Bible tells us to "rejoice with others who rejoice" (Romans 12:15).

**Attitude:** Have you noticed how your attitude can affect what happens? Remember, you can always choose your attitude.

**Compassion:** If someone is sad, do you make an effort to speak comforting words to her? A simple "I'm sorry you're going through that. Is there anything I can do to help?" goes a long way. Most importantly, it reveals the beauty in your heart.

**Confidence:** There is a big difference between being confident and being stuck-up. Confidence comes from being sure of yourself and appreciating the gifts God has given you. Being stuck-up is having a high opinion of yourself and taking credit for the gifts God has given you.

**Servant's heart:** I am shocked at the number of people who have never been taught to look out for the needy. I have watched kids and teenagers rudely brush past elderly people—practically knocking them over—when heading through a door. If you see people in need, elderly or not, offer to help them. A servant's heart is one of the most beautiful character qualities there is.

**Treating your family well:** There is nothing more unattractive than a girl snapping sarcastically at her parents or her brothers and sisters in public. If this is a problem for you, learn to hold your tongue, take a deep breath, and talk calmly when the time is right.

**Being yourself:** Most girls are so busy trying to be like someone else that they forget the person that God created them to be. Don't be afraid to be you! You are a unique creation of God.

**Faith:** A girl who loves Jesus more than life can't help but shine from the inside out. She will brighten every room she enters, and her glow for Christ will be contagious.

## What About You?

1. Which of these beauty secrets do you already use in your daily life?

2. Which of these beauty secrets do you need to start putting into practice?

# Wise Words from High School Girls

We asked a group of high school girls the following question: *What advice would you give tween girls about appearance and body image? What words of wisdom could you offer about the pressures our culture puts on girls to look a certain way and fit a narrow standard of beauty?*

## Sam, 14

Personally, I've had a lot of struggles with body image throughout middle school—being too tall, being thicker than all the other girls, a lot of stuff. Something that really helps me is to look through verses about "who you are in Christ" (new creation, His workmanship). Instead of trying to conform to the world's type of beauty, realize you are already beautiful in God's eyes and that you are His special creation.

## Riley, 18

I have struggled with self-image for a long time. I always compared myself to others and thought I was never pretty enough. The more I struggled, the more I felt alone. One night I laid it all out to God. I cried and asked for His help. It was that moment that I knew I wasn't alone. God made us all exactly how He wanted us to be. No other opinions matter except for His. So what if you don't look like the models in magazines? God loves you unconditionally and calls you His child. The standards don't matter. You are beautiful because God made you! You must remember that in the hardest times of your life. The times when you're struggling to see yourself as pretty and worthy, turn your face to God. You are worthy to Him, and that's the only thing that matters! Don't let anyone tell you you're not.

## Mittie, 14

Do not worry about what is on the outside—worry about what is on the inside. You are made in God's image, and He has made you beautiful just the way you are. The culture has set a standard of beauty that is not true. Just because you are not skinny or short or tall doesn't mean you are not pretty.

## Caroline, 15

All girls need to know that God says we are "fearfully and wonderfully made" (Psalm 139:14 NIV), and despite what anyone says, we are incredibly beautiful in God's eyes. I have certainly struggled with trying to look a certain way in hopes that I would feel more beautiful, but as hard as I tried to be what the world said was beautiful, I was never satisfied. I never seemed to measure up to all the beautiful girls I was trying to be like. God showed me that I was beautiful the way I was, and I didn't have to try to fit into the world's narrow standard of beauty.

## Erin, 17

My biggest advice for girls regarding body image is to find your confidence in the Lord. I have struggled with comparing myself to celebrities, older girls in a different stage of life, and girls my age. I prayed about finding peace with who I was, and I continue to pray every night about this issue. Remember that God crafted every part of you specifically and purposefully. Your hair, your eyes, your personality, EVERYTHING was designed by God to be just how it is. Be confident that you were designed specifically, and nothing about you is a mistake. Finding confidence not in worldly standards but in God's eyes was, and is, key for me.

## Allie, 18

Our world has created one "perfect" body image, and if we don't meet it, they are not afraid to let us know. God, however, sees the beauty in everything and thinks that you are worth more than gold no matter your size, hair length, or skin color. This has been one of my biggest struggles through all my years of school, and looking back I wish that I would've listened to Him all along. The hurt that I felt for constantly trying to fit that "perfect" body image is like a never-ending race with no champion. God sees us as more than gold. If the Creator of the whole world thinks that of you, then our culture's opinion of you should not even cross your mind.

## Tate, 14

I used to think I had to look "perfect"—that word always got to me. I had to have the *perfect* hair, *perfect* clothes, and the *perfect* body. I soon realized that being perfect is hard, and it doesn't matter because the only person who is perfect is the Lord. There is no need to strive to be perfect because you will never be perfect in anyone else's eyes but God's. God looks at us as though we are perfect because it is in Him we are made beautifully, wonderfully, and perfectly.

# Never Ever

Never ever define your worth by your reflection in the mirror.

Never ever think you're ugly.

Never ever believe you can't change for the better.

Never ever forget that you are wonderfully made.

Never ever think that you have to look like girls in fashion magazines, on social media, or on TV.

Never ever wish you could be someone else.

Never ever say, "I hate myself."

Never ever define your worth by what other people say.

Never ever accept the lie that if you aren't "popular" you aren't important.

Never ever change who you are just to fit in.

# Dear Daughter,

You and I had a really bad day yesterday. We had a fight—a doozy of a fight—over hair.

Yes, hair.

We had been busy all day, getting school supplies and running errands. That afternoon, you and Dad went swimming. You got back in just enough time to take a shower and get ready for a company picnic. Or at least I thought you had enough time. Your dad and I gave you a countdown—twenty minutes until we needed to leave, fifteen minutes, ten . . . you get the idea. When I went into your bathroom to check on your progress, you were in tears. Your hair was half-wet and partially straightened. When I told you it was time to leave and you'd just have to put your half-dry, not-so-straight hair in a ponytail and get dressed, you lost it. Meltdown in progress. You cried and yelled. I yelled back. It was ugly.

Why am I reminding you of this terrible, awful, very bad meltdown? Because of what caused it—your *hair*. You are in a place right now where you think you have to look perfect. Your hair is only one example. Your clothes. Your shoes. Your backpack. Your jewelry. All of it has to be perfect. You worry *a lot* about how you look. And I think I understand why.

You are growing up in a culture that tells you what you're supposed to look like. And it's stressful! You're supposed to have pretty hair. Nice skin. (No zits allowed!) You're supposed to be skinny. You're supposed to be average height—not too tall and not too short. And of course, you're supposed to wear the latest fashion and look good in everything, and you're supposed to buy those clothes at the cool stores. Where do you hear these messages? You hear them everywhere. TV commercials. Friends. Ads on your apps. Social media. Just a few days ago, you were frustrated because an outfit you were trying on didn't match the ad you saw.

The world around you tells you that your worth as a person is based on how you look on the outside. The cute girl gets the cute guy, right? That's what the TV shows and movies tell you. Think about it: Have you ever seen an average-looking princess in a fairy tale? Have you ever seen an average girl be the most popular in a movie? Nope.

I need to tell you something really, really important: *what you see on TV and movies and ads and social media isn't real.*

When you get a little older, I want to show you the power of Photoshop. That's a computer program that allows you to alter photographs. You can remove pimples, take away muffin tops, change hair color, and even insert a person into the picture with you. I want to show you exactly what designers and photographers do to pictures. I want you to see for yourself that what you see on billboards and magazines *IS NOT REAL*. It's all phony. Fake. Pretend. Made-up. False. Bogus. Fantasyland.

And the idea that your worth is based on your outward appearance? That's bogus too.

Do you remember the conversation we had in the car last night, after the hair meltdown? We talked about your friends and your not-so-favorite people. I asked you why you liked your friends. You talked about them being funny and sweet and kind and safe. And when I asked you about the girls you didn't like, you said they were mean and rude and gossiped too much.

Do you remember what I pointed out? You never *once* mentioned their hair. Or clothes. Or weight. What made you like people—or not like them—had *nothing* to do with what was on the outside. You didn't care if they had the right clothes or cool sunglasses. What mattered to you was the stuff inside—what was in their hearts.

Over the next few years, your body is going to wig out on you. That's a part of growing up. You won't feel good about how you look, even when you look awesome. When you have those bad self-esteem days (and EVERYONE has them—even the prettiest girl in school), I hope you will look back at this letter and read it again. I hope you remember that what you look like doesn't change how important and valuable and loved and cherished and amazing you are. I want you to remember that what makes you amazing is what's in your heart, not what's on your body.

*Love, Mom*

## Can You See Beauty?

Unscramble the letters to see how God made you . . .

**ULBUTIEAF** _____

**NUQUIE** _____

**MKABRELAER** _____

**WDOFULERN** _____

**DARAINT** _____

**URPE** _____

**VELOLY** _____

**DORXEINAYRTAR** _____

Celebrate how God has made you: *beautiful, unique, remarkable, wonderful, radiant, pure, lovely, and extraordinary*! He created you just the way you are, and He loves you more than you could ever imagine!

# Think This, Not That

## by Tami Overhauser

One of the first things you do in the morning is look in the mirror. Why not start the day by getting your thoughts rolling in the right direction? Replace any negative thoughts with God's Word and see if it changes how you look at yourself! Hopefully you'll start to "reflect" a new and positive attitude about how God made you.

Look up the following verses this week. Think about the truths they represent every time you glance in the mirror:

You are "fearfully and wonderfully made." (Psalm 139:14 NIV)

You are created in God's image. (Genesis 1:27)

You are cared for. (Luke 12:22-24)

You are the work of God's hand. (Isaiah 64:8)

You are beautiful. (Ecclesiastes 3:11 NIV)

You are a child of God. (John 1:12)

You are "dearly loved." (Colossians 3:12 NIV)

You are infinitely valuable to God. (Luke 12:7)

You are beautiful from the inside out. (1 Peter 3:3-4)

You are loved with an everlasting love. (Jeremiah 31:3)

# THAT THING YOU DO

# Cheerleader, Rah

## by Vicki Courtney

It was a simple, white T-shirt with a stick figure of a girl holding pom-poms and a two-word slogan printed underneath: "Cheerleader, rah." I think I may have worn it every day in the summer after making the middle school cheer squad, except for when my mom made me peel it off and put it in the washer. Oh, and don't forget the megaphone necklace and matching earrings. I guess you could say I was proud of being elected a cheerleader. I wasn't that great at dance, and I couldn't sing. I stunk at art and wasn't into drama. I was smart, but not a straight-A student. Cheerleading was my thing, and it made me feel good to have something I did well. The problem is, it was my everything. My identity was wrapped up in being a cheerleader.

What is your thing? There's nothing wrong with being proud of your gifts and talents, but you can go overboard when you base your worth on them. How do you know if this is a problem? Ask yourself this one simple question about that thing that makes you feel special: *What if it went away?*

What if you don't make the team or the honor roll? What if you don't make a good grade on the vocabulary quiz or get cast in a lead role in the upcoming school play? What if you have to sit on the bench during the big game, or you get picked last for a group project in school? What if you get injured and can't compete? What if you lose the one board game you always win—to your little brother? What if you are no longer the smart girl, the athletic girl, the trendy girl, the funny girl, or the popular girl? Apart from your accomplishments and titles, would you still feel good about yourself? I hope so.

I knew I had a problem when I didn't make the cheerleading squad the next year and my self-esteem took a dive. I felt like a nobody without the uniform and saddle oxfords. And that "Cheerleader, rah" T-shirt went straight into the Goodwill pile. I couldn't even bring myself to keep it for a nightshirt. I felt lost. If I wasn't Vicki the cheerleader, then who was I? The problem with basing your worth on your titles and accomplishments is that you set a trap for yourself. Eventually, the trap will spring.

Just as I learned, a title, honor, trophy, or award can be temporary. If you count on it for your self-worth, then when it disappears, you will feel worthless.

Maybe cheerleading isn't your thing, or maybe you haven't even found your thing yet. That's perfectly okay. You're still young and have plenty of time to discover your gifts and talents. What's important is that you know the purpose of the gifts and talents God gives you. God never intended our gifts and talents to define us and be the basis for our self-esteem. First Peter 4:10 says, "Each of you should use whatever gift you have received to serve others, as faithful stewards of God's grace in its various forms" (NIV). We can't take credit for our gifts because they come from God. For that reason, our worth shouldn't come from our gifts and talents, but rather from the One who gave us the gifts and talents. God never changes, so if we look to Him to define our worth, our worth will not waver.

But don't miss the second part of the verse. Our gifts were given to us for the purpose of serving others and pointing them to God's amazing grace. God is not concerned with whether or not our gifts translate into wins, successes, trophies, certificates, or pats on the back. His main concern is that we use our gifts to make Him shine . . . not ourselves.

If I could go back and talk to my younger self when I was sobbing into my pillow after not being elected cheerleader, I would tell that girl that there is only one title that can bring you lasting worth. It's not Vicki the cheerleader. It's Vicki the forgiven, much-loved child of God. Who needs a silly T-shirt that says, "Cheerleader, rah" when God's name is written on your heart?

## What About You?

1. Is your worth tied to your titles or accomplishments? If they went away, would it be hard to feel good about yourself?

2. Describe a time when you didn't succeed, win, or perform well and you felt like a nobody.

3. Read 1 Peter 4:10 again. Where do our gifts come from? What is the purpose of our gifts?

4. What are some ways you can use your gifts to serve others and point them to God?

## What talent or gift has God given YOU?

Scan for Video Answers!

# Dare to Be Brave

We all have dreams, but sometimes the fear of failure holds us back.

If you knew you wouldn't fail, what dream would you chase?

Become a famous artist.
   Lila, 10

Become a ballerina.
   Callie, 8

Be in *The Nutcracker.*
   Abbi, 8

I would dance.
   Olivia, 12

I would ride a shark in the ocean.
   Clarissa, 11

Play lacrosse.
   Reagan, 10

Write a book.
   Spencer, 11

I would be an Olympic volleyball player
   or maybe an astronaut.
   Grace, 13

Be a soccer player and a singer.
   Mazie, 12

Be a superhero.
   Brooke, 11

Finish college in three years.
   Nova, 11

Be a midwife!
   Abigail, 10

Help bring world peace.
   Olivia, 10

Be a police dog trainer.
   Lydia, 9

Have a family and be a vet,
   maybe even a marine biologist.
   Ella, 10

Be a fashion designer.
   Lacey, 8

I would get my master's in interior design and have a home-design TV show.
   Emma, 12

Eat a hot dog in three bites!
   Mae Beth, 9

Be an actress, write a book, and be a mom.
   Elsie, 12

I'm a foster child, and I want to be the first in my family to go to college.
   Logen, 12

Become a kindergarten teacher and a pro tennis player.
   Skylar, 10

Be a librarian.
   Lindsay, 9

Be a missionary.
   Madison, 10

Be a veterinarian.
   Becca, 11

Be a professional surfer!
   Nicole, 8

Be a camp counselor.
   Annika, 10

I want to be an architect.
   Delaney, 11

I want to be kind to everyone, but sometimes it's really hard.
Emma Grace, 11

Become president of the United States.
Paige Abigail, 9

# What About You?

1. What would you do if you weren't afraid of failure?

2. Why do you think we let fear hold us back?

I can do all things through Christ who strengthens me.—Philippians 4:13 NKJV

Let your light shine before others. —Matthew 5:16 ESV

Delight yourself in the LORD, and he will give you the desires of your heart.—Psalm 37:4 ESV

The LORD directs the steps of the godly. He delights in every detail of their lives. —Psalm 37:23 NLT

The heart of man plans his way, but the LORD establishes his steps.—Proverbs 16:9 ESV

Commit your way to the LORD: trust in him, and he will act.—Psalm 37:5 ESV

Be strong and courageous.—Joshua 1:9 ESV

The righteous are bold as a lion.—Proverbs 28:1 ESV

# The Emotional Roller Coaster

## by Meredith Derry

One day you're happy, but the next day you're sad or angry. Some days you have no idea what you feel! Sound familiar? Sometimes in certain stages of life, we feel like our emotions are all over the place. We can feel overwhelmed, confused, and even out of control. God created our emotions, and it is a gift to be able to feel things deeply. However, it is also important to understand why at certain ages our emotions can go up and down so dramatically—kind of like a roller coaster! There are some ways we can learn to control our emotions in these challenging times. God gives us wisdom and truth in His Word to stand on during this stage of life.

From the time girls are nine years old until around fifteen years old, their bodies are growing and changing—and so are their emotions. This can be a difficult and confusing time because we can have many feelings all at once. However, this is just part of growing up, and there are some steps we can take to make the roller-coaster ride a little bit smoother.

The first step to take when you're having a lot of different emotions is to figure out what you are feeling. Are you feeling hurt? Or lonely? Maybe you're feeling sad or afraid. If your little brother is annoying you, you probably feel frustrated and angry. If you did something wrong, you might even feel guilty.

Once you know what you are feeling, find someone you trust, and share your heart with that person. This may be a parent, someone who helps in your children's or student ministry at church, or a teacher or coach. Our feelings tell us what we need, so you can work together with an adult you trust to figure out what your feelings mean. Don't forget, we can always talk to God about what we're feeling. If you still need help, writing about your emotions in a journal is a great solution as well.

Because of how God made us, when we don't share our feelings, we react like an erupting volcano. When we stuff our feelings down and don't talk about them, it's like adding more pressure to the lava in that volcano. Just as a volcano suddenly erupts, our emotions can "explode" as well. We may begin to rage at our families or friends, treating them very unkindly, or we may start crying and not be able to stop. We may even hurt someone with our words and actions. Talking about what we are feeling with someone we trust and figuring out what we need allows our emotions to come out slowly, lessening the pressure of the "lava" and giving us more control over our emotions. It also gives our family and friends a chance to know us better, creating stronger relationships with them. This allows us to see how loved we are.

During seasons of life when there is so much change happening in our bodies, minds, and emotions, we may have to practice patience, trusting that God will give us everything we need to get us through this stage. God is faithful to give us patience and wisdom so that we can be kind to others and also kind to ourselves as we grow and change. In James 1:2–4, God teaches us that tough stages of life can make us more like Christ. The tween and teenage years are difficult, but the roller coaster of emotions doesn't have to be a crazy, out-of-control ride—especially when you take Jesus with you on the roller coaster!

## What About You?

1. Do you sometimes feel like your emotions are out of control?

2. Is there a specific time of day or situation that almost always stirs up your emotions (example: right before bed when you're tired or right before dinner when you're hungry)?

3. Do you share your feelings with people you trust, or do you hold them inside? Why?

4. Do you talk with God about your feelings? Why or why not?

# Wise Words from High School Girls

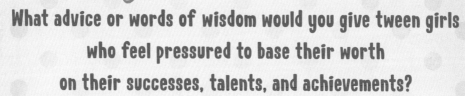

## What advice or words of wisdom would you give tween girls who feel pressured to base their worth on their successes, talents, and achievements?

**Sam, 14**

Basing my worth on my talents has always been hard for me because I had a period of time in which I didn't have a "thing" (an elective or a hobby). I felt pretty worthless when I saw other people enjoying themselves. It made me sad. What helped was to remember that my worth is in Christ. He does not base His approval or His love on how good you are at sports or art or music. His love is unconditional. Through that realization of accepting God's love as my worth, I found my "thing" was loving God as much as I could.

**Mittie, 14**

Do not place your worth in things of this world like talents, hobbies, or friends. All of those things are temporary in life. We need to focus on eternal things like our relationship with God. I used to struggle with getting caught up in sports, not even remembering God gave me talents to honor Him.

## Erin, 18

Ephesians 2:8-10: These are verses I have been reading since middle school, and they help keep this issue in perspective. It says: "For it is by grace you have been saved, through faith—and this is not from yourselves, it is the gift of God—not by works, so that no one can boast. For we are God's handiwork, created in Christ Jesus to do good works, which God prepared in advance for us to do" (NIV).

## Alle, 18

God tells us many times in the Bible that everything on this earth is temporary. He will not look at you and say, "Good job! You made the basketball team!" or say, "You had the best voice out of your whole choir!" God cares more about the impact you made on this earth for Him. All of your earthly treasures and desires will vanish when you get to heaven. So instead of wasting your time on achieving earthly talents, successes, and achievements, we should focus on living for the One who made us and following His plan for us on this earth instead of our own.

### Tate, 14

When you get older you start to find your worth in almost everything around you. The popular girls, boys, grades, and even sports. This was one of the hardest lessons I had to learn in middle school. I found myself needing the approval of the mean girls and needing a boy to tell me I am pretty when in reality their approval does not mean anything compared to what the Lord thinks of us. So when we find our worth in someone other than Christ, we are telling God He isn't good enough. If I would have known that going into middle school, I would have been a much more joyful person who doesn't care what others think—someone who knows where true worth comes from.

# QUIZ

## In This Corner (Humility v. Pride)

### by Vicki Courtney

Every time you see the word *humble* in the Bible, it is talking about acting with humility. Everything about being a Christian is connected to the idea of humility—from loving God to loving others. So, what is it exactly? Simply put, humility is having a correct understanding of your true worth (or value) in Christ, and not in yourself. It means not having too high an opinion of yourself (or thinking you're "all that") and being aware that God is responsible for all the good things He does through you. Basically, humility is giving God the credit for all the good things about you and in your life. At the same time, humility also means not having too low an opinion of yourself and understanding that through Him, you are a priceless treasure!

Humility puts others' needs above our own. Jesus Christ was the perfect (literally!) example when He went to the cross and died for our sins. Not only that, but He served those around Him while He was on earth by healing them, listening to their problems, and even washing their feet. Talk about humility! The perfect, holy God of the universe came to love and serve sinful humans. Whoa! That is, in a word, humility!

In the following section, rate yourself on a scale of 1 to 10 based on how you typically act. The closer to 1 you circle, the closer you typically behave to the sentence on the left. The closer to 10 you circle, the closer you typically behave to the sentence on the right.

| | | |
|---|---|---|
| Your way isn't always the best. | 1 2 ~~3~~ 4 5 6 7 8 9 10 | Your way is the only way. |
| You think of others as better than you. | 1 ~~2~~ 3 4 5 6 7 8 9 10 | You think you're better than others. |
| You ask for forgiveness when you do something wrong. | ~~1~~ 2 3 4 5 6 7 8 9 10 | You only say you're sorry when someone tells you to. |
| You thank God for the blessing when you make a good grade. | ~~1~~ 2 3 4 5 6 7 8 9 10 | You take all the credit for your good grades and intelligence. |
| You would gladly give up a Saturday to help others. | 1 2 3 4 5 ~~6~~ 7 8 9 10 | You find excuses not to help out. |
| You let others give the answers in class, even if you know them. | ~~1~~ 2 3 4 5 6 7 8 9 10 | You feel the need to prove you know all the answers. |
| You accept advice when others point out areas you need to improve. | 1 2 3 4 5 ~~6~~ 7 8 9 10 | You get mad or upset when others point out areas you need to improve. |
| You thank God for athletic ability when you do well in sports. | ~~1~~ 2 3 4 5 6 7 8 9 10 | You show off and take all the credit for your athletic ability. |
| You want to please God more than people. | 1 ~~2~~ 3 4 5 6 7 8 9 10 | You're more concerned with getting people to like you than pleasing God. |
| You accept your part of the blame in disagreements and fights. | 1 2 3 4 ~~5~~ 6 7 8 9 10 | You get defensive and point out the faults of others. |

*Now, total up the numbers you circled to see what corner you're in! How did you do?*

## Knockout:
If you scored between 10 and 39, you seek to live in a way that gives God credit. You strive to serve others and recognize that all your talent and ability comes from God. Though you tend to make these wise choices now, don't assume you always will. It is incredibly easy to slip into making prideful choices. Pray, pray, pray!

## Dancing Around the Ring:
If you scored between 40 and 70, you are in good company with most other people! Like everyone, you sometimes give in to pride. But the good news is, you are at least trying to make the right choices. You know the right ways to live, but sometimes have a hard time living them out. Developing humility is a lifelong process. What you can do, however, is practice changing your heart in some of the areas where you scored the highest. Pray first, and ask God for the strength and ability to choose humility over pride. It is definitely not easy, and certainly not natural, so it will take some divine doing! When you begin to see improvement, remember to give God the credit and praise Him for helping you to look more like Jesus.

## Down for the Count:
If you scored between 71 and 100, you are having a really hard time choosing humility over pride. Pray and ask God to show you the "yuck" in your heart when you act prideful. Begin by taking three of the above statements where you scored an eight, nine, or ten, and when those situations come up, pray for God to help you choose humility instead of pride. Be warned! When you pray for something like that, He usually answers in unexpected ways and gives you MANY opportunities to practice!

# God Sees Everything

## by Vicki Courtney

*For a man's ways are before the LORD's eyes, and He considers all his paths.—Proverbs 5:21*

Imagine if one day at school the principal announced on the intercom that there were hidden cameras all around the school. Now imagine that the principal said someone would be watching TV monitors in a control room throughout the day and writing down students' names when they misbehaved. Then, at the end of the day, the control room operators would turn the list of names in to the principal, and each name would be announced over the loudspeaker—along with a list of ways each student misbehaved. That would be crazy, right?

Well, believe it or not, the police department in one wacky British town did something similar in an effort to cut back on crime. They set up 158 cameras around the city and fitted seven of them with loudspeakers. Control room operators would watch their assigned areas and step in if there was any trouble.

One young man who lived in the town was riding his bike and pedaled into an area of a park where bikes were not allowed. All of a sudden a loud voice came from one of the speakers overhead and said, "Would the young man on the bike please get off and walk, as he is riding in a pedestrian area?" The surprised boy stopped and looked around, confused and unsure where the voice came from. When he realized the mystery voice was referring to him, he immediately got off his bike and walked it away from the park area, his face bright red with embarrassment as surprised onlookers watched him.

Proverbs 5:21 tells us God has the ability to see everything we do. Nothing is hidden from His sight. Fortunately He doesn't sit in a control room all day and scream at us over a loudspeaker when we misbehave. Or take our names down and turn them in to our parents! He gives us the freedom to choose our paths—even when we decide to go off course. He is patient and loving, nudging us to get back on track when we stray. I don't know about you, but knowing God loves me that way makes me want to obey Him. It would be hard to love a God who yelled at me every time I messed up.

It kind of reminds me of my sixth-grade math teacher, Mrs. Cooper, who caught me passing a note to one of my friends in class. She intercepted the note and proceeded to read it out loud to the class. It was embarrassing enough since I told my friend I thought Steve Miller was super cute, and he was sitting right there on the front row. But here's the worst part: I also said something about Mrs. Cooper being the meanest teacher in the entire universe. After she read my note to the class, she folded it back up, handed it to me, and sent me to the office to read the note to the principal. Joy.

You may wonder what my next punishment was. The principal made me write one hundred times: "I will not pass notes in class. I will show respect to my teacher." Ouch. I mean, oh sure, I probably deserved to get in trouble, but did Mrs. Cooper have to embarrass me in front of the entire class? And in front of Steve Miller? So yeah, I still think she is the meanest teacher in the entire universe, but you can bet I wasn't going to write it in a note after that! In fact, let's

hope she doesn't read it in this book—I'm still afraid she might hunt me down and try to send me to the office!

Take a minute to thank God for being patient and loving even when you make mistakes. Ask Him to send loving reminders when you stray to nudge you back onto the right path.

# What About You?

1. Can you think of something you did wrong this past week? Maybe you talked back to your mother, gossiped about a friend, or told a lie to your brother. What was it?

2. Do you think God knew about that sin when it happened? Did He shout at you over a loudspeaker?

3. Can you think of a time when someone (such as a parent or teacher) was patient with you when you made a mistake and corrected you in a loving manner? Who was it? What happened?

4. Do you believe God is patient with you when you make a mistake and corrects you in a loving manner?

# What to Do (and NOT Do) When You Make a Mistake

### by Vicki Courtney

*People who conceal their sins will not prosper, but if they confess and turn from them, they will receive mercy. Blessed are those who fear to do wrong, but the stubborn are headed for serious trouble.*
Proverbs 28:13–14 NLT

When I was about five years old, I stole something. My mom stopped by the drugstore to pick up some things, and while she was shopping, I asked if I could go look at the toys on the toy aisle. "Go look, but we can't buy anything today," she said as I raced off. For what seemed like hours (it was probably more like five minutes!), I paced the toy aisle making a mental list of all the toys I would buy if I had a million dollars. I was looking at one toy in particular when I heard my mother calling my name and telling me it was time to go. It was a little army man with a parachute; throw it in the air, and the parachute opens up, so the little army man slowly floats down. I really wanted to see if it would work, and without thinking, I put it in my pocket and raced to the checkout to meet my mom.

I remember on the ride home feeling very guilty, but I didn't say anything. When we finally pulled into the garage, my mom told me I could play outside for a few minutes until dinner. Finally! I had my chance to see if the parachute would really work. I took it out of my pocket and slowly unwound the rubber band that secured the parachute. Once it was ready, I climbed up in my tree house again and dropped it down. And what do you know? It worked! It really worked! About that time my mom walked outside and saw me dropping it from the tree house again. "Where did you get that?" she asked. *Uh-oh, busted.* "Uhhhh," I stuttered, "at the drugstore." She gave me a suspicious look and said, "I don't remember paying for it at the checkout. How did you get it?" At this point the floodgates burst, and the tears started flowing. "I promise I didn't mean to steal it!" I cried.

My mom handled it pretty well and told me to get in the car. She headed right back to the drugstore and told me that I had to tell the store manager that I had taken the toy without paying for it. I was so scared on the way over. Finally we pulled into a parking spot, and it was time to face my fear. Mom went with me and assured me that I would feel much better once I told the truth. I had folded the parachute back up as neatly as I could and wrapped the rubber band back around it to hold it tightly in place. My mom asked to speak to the manager while I held it tightly in my hand and stared down at the ground. I was so ashamed. When the manager finally approached and asked, "How can I help you?" the tears began to flow again. I handed him the parachute toy and told him through my tears that I had taken it without paying for it but that I was really sorry. He was nice about the whole thing and told me that while stealing was very wrong, he was proud that I had decided to do the right thing and return it.

Of course, I wish I had listened to my conscience sooner. I knew it was wrong and wanted to tell my mother to turn the car around so I could take it back. But I didn't. And you know what? As fun as it was to try the parachute out and see it float down from the tree house, I didn't really enjoy it much after the first try, because I knew deep down inside that it wasn't really mine to enjoy. Once I had finally confessed my sin and returned the toy, I felt a huge sense of relief sweep over me.

No matter how big or small the sin may be, we can't cover it up or pretend it never happened. We will all trip up from time to time, and when we do, we need to confess our sin to God first. Then we need to make it right with those who have been affected by our selfishness. The best way to avoid sin is to listen to your conscience (that little voice inside that tells you when something is wrong). And when we do mess up, the best way to handle it is to confess and determine not to make that mistake again.

Pray and ask God to give you a tender conscience when it comes to sin. Pray that your conscience will keep you from committing a sin when you are tempted. If necessary, go ahead and confess to Him right now if there is something on your conscience that you need to share. He's listening and ready to give you mercy.

## What About You?

1. When I confessed my sin of stealing, who gave me mercy?

2. If I had been stubborn and chosen not to tell the truth when my mother asked me where I got the toy, how might it have led me toward serious trouble in the future? (Hint: See Proverbs 28:13–14.)

3. Have you ever attempted to conceal your sin?

4. Did you end up confessing it to anyone? If not, do you wish you had done so? (It's never too late!)

# The Problem with Exaggerating

## by Meredith Derry

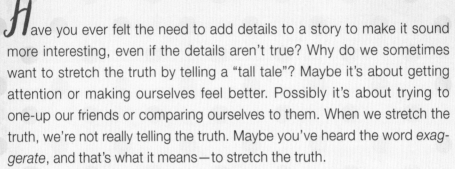

Have you ever felt the need to add details to a story to make it sound more interesting, even if the details aren't true? Why do we sometimes want to stretch the truth by telling a "tall tale"? Maybe it's about getting attention or making ourselves feel better. Possibly it's about trying to one-up our friends or comparing ourselves to them. When we stretch the truth, we're not really telling the truth. Maybe you've heard the word *exaggerate*, and that's what it means—to stretch the truth.

Let's start by thinking about some reasons why we might exaggerate. When we exaggerate, we may notice our friends becoming fascinated with our stories. It makes us feel pretty important when people seem interested in us and start to believe what we say. We may even find that certain people talk to us more or we feel more accepted by our friends when we stretch the truth.

However, if we take a closer look at why we do it, we might discover that we exaggerate because we're insecure. We wonder if who we are and what we say is worth listening to. We worry that no one will want to hear about our lives, at least not without turning our stories into something exciting or dramatic. We want people to like us and to be interested in what happens to us. We're afraid they will stop listening if our lives sound boring.

Take a few moments to think about what happens when we exaggerate or say things that aren't completely true. Does it help people trust us more or cause them to trust us less? When we always tell the truth, our friends and family learn to trust what we have to say instead of wondering if we are telling a lie.

Think of it this way: Imagine you are building a tower of trust with your words, and every time you tell the truth, you stack another building block onto the structure. When someone catches you exaggerating or lying, all the blocks fall to the ground and you have to start building the tower all over again. This is a picture of what happens with the words we say. When we are honest, we build trust with our family and friends. But when we lie or stretch the truth, our tower of trust falls to the ground, and we have to rebuild it.

God tells us throughout His Word that we honor Him when we tell the truth. He warns us in Psalm 34:13 to keep our tongue from evil and our mouth from speaking lies. In Proverbs 12:22, we learn that He despises lying lips but delights in those who tell the truth.

It is so important for us to be honest. When we share what's really happening in our lives, we give people a chance to get to know us and build lasting relationships. When we choose to be honest, we earn the trust of family, friends, and even kids we barely know at school. When people trust us, they will listen to what we have to say. Our words should be used to speak truth, love, and hope into people's lives. From now on, let your words point others to Jesus, who is "the way, the truth, and the life" (John 14:6).

## What About You?

1. Do you struggle with exaggerating? Are you tempted to stretch the truth sometimes?

2. Have you ever lost the trust of someone you cared about because you told a lie?

3. How did you earn their trust back?

4. Why is it so important for us to be known as truthful people?

# Dear Daughter,

Just a little while ago, I watched you beam with pride at your school's award ceremony. I worried that you might be left out—and there you were—winning! It feels really great when you get recognized for your hard work, even when you grow up!

I remember being your age (yes, I was a kid too!) and being at my own awards ceremony at school. I won a few awards. Actually, I got a bunch. I think your grandma still has a few up in her attic! As I got older, I got used to getting awards. I got used to good grades. In fact, I felt disappointed in myself when I didn't ace every test or homework assignment. I thought my parents would be disappointed in me. I worried my teachers wouldn't like me anymore. I was the good kid. I was supposed to make good grades, and I began to think that my worth was wrapped up in what I did. If I got good grades, I felt good about myself. If I got bad grades, I felt horrible.

Your dad and I have taught you to do your best. That's okay. And it's okay to be competitive. You get that from your dad! But I want to tell you something important: it's okay to be average sometimes. You don't have to do anything special for your dad and me to love you. I wish my parents had told me that. Here's something else you need to remember: you can't be great at everything. You aren't a failure if you can't remember all the states and their capitals. That just means you need to study a little more next time.

When you get older, you'll be tempted to be involved in everything—soccer, band, yearbook, student council, youth group stuff. If you do too much, though, you won't be able to do your best at any of them. That's why we as your parents say no sometimes. We are trying to teach you to do a few things well instead of a bunch of things not-so-well.

Whatever you get really good at, whether it's cheering or being a good friend, remember that your worth isn't based on the things you do. You are valuable because God created you. More about that later. Until then, keep doing your best, but don't worry about being the best.

Love, Mom

# QUIZ: Get Real!

## Casey Courtney

Everyone hates a fake—so start getting honest with yourself and God! Take this quiz and find out if the real you needs a spiritual makeover. What would you do in each of the following scenarios?

**1. It's the end of the day, and you haven't had a quiet time with God. You . . .**
a) say a quick good-night prayer and hit the sheets.
b) make some quality time with God before you snooze.
c) don't really think about it and text your friends before catching some z's.

**2. One of your teachers makes a comment in class about God being make-believe. You . . .**
a) stay silent, hoping he won't remember you are a Christian.
b) politely share why you believe in God, even though your teacher might think less of you.
c) join in, even though that's not how you really feel inside.

**3. Your best friend wants to copy your homework. You . . .**
a) tell her you didn't know how to do the homework and only guessed at the answers.
b) decline and let her know dishonesty is wrong, but you'll be happy to help her study.
c) give her your homework and tell her to copy fast!

**4. It's a Friday-night sleepover, and your friends are secretly watching a movie they know their parents wouldn't approve of. You . . .**
a) pretend you're sick and tell them you have to go home.
b) tell them you can't hang out with them if they're going to go against their parents' wishes and encourage them to do something else instead.
c) watch it—you have really been wanting to see that movie!

**5. You're sitting at church when the most unpopular girl sits down in the chair next to you. You . . .**
a) stay where you are but convince your friends to come sit with you so you don't have to sit next to her by yourself.
b) ask her how her week was, try to get to know her a little better, and invite her over after church.
c) pretend you have a phone call and go to the back to see where the cute guys are sitting.

**6. It's Monday morning, and you forgot to do your homework because you went out of town with your family. You . . .**

a) stretch the truth and tell your teacher you had a "family emergency." I mean, your parents' car did run out of gas on the way out of town.

b) tell your teacher you completely forgot and ask if she will let you turn it in tomorrow morning.

c) borrow your friend's homework and copy it quickly before class.

**7. You're at a friend's birthday party, and girls are talking badly about one of your friends who's not there. You . . .**

a) don't participate in the conversation but stick around anyway.

b) let them know they are being unkind and excuse yourself.

c) join in the fun. It's not that big of a deal!

**IF YOU ANSWERED MOSTLY A:** Get a backbone. You know what's right but sometimes have a hard time standing up for what you believe. Find a Christian friend who can keep you accountable as well as encourage you to stand up for God. Get your approval from God and not your friends, and He will give you the courage to do what's right, even when everyone around you is making wrong choices.

**IF YOU ANSWERED MOSTLY B:** You get it—congratulations! You balance real life with godly values, and you're not afraid to stand up for what you believe. Your friends know you're not ashamed to be a Christian, and you stick to your Christian standards. Stay strong and continue to put God first in your life.

**IF YOU ANSWERED MOSTLY C:** Get a spiritual makeover. You crave the approval of your friends, which often leads to wrong choices or situations that leave you unsatisfied. Sin can be fun for a season, but eventually the separation from God leaves us feeling empty and alone. It's never too late to ask God to be the center of your life. Spend time with Him daily, and He will change your heart and desires. Eventually it won't matter what others are doing; you will realize you have a deeper peace when you obey God instead.

# Losing Isn't Easy

## Rachel Prochnow

I can remember the crowning moment at the pageant like it was yesterday. "And then there were two! One of these two ladies will represent Texas for the next year," the announcer's voice boomed over the microphone. This was the moment I had worked so hard for. Sweat began to form on my forehead. On stage, my hands clutched the hands of the other girl. I was confident I had this in the bag; I had prepared so well, competed flawlessly.

"And the winner is Brandy Phillips!"

That wasn't my name.

My heart dropped. I fought back tears as I hugged the new winner.

We've all been there: the time when we *didn't* win. Maybe you wanted to win the reading competition at school, but another girl had read three more books than you. Maybe you didn't make the top volleyball team but got put on the lower team. Either way, rejection is tough to deal with. Something I have learned is that God can use rejection for good. It can actually make you a *better* person. I lost quite a bit growing up. And God used that to teach me some valuable lessons. Here are some of the lessons I want to share with you.

## 1. Whether You Win or Lose, God Still Loves You

Guess what—God loves you regardless of whether or not you come home with the first-place trophy. His love for you stands strong no matter what you accomplish. His love is what saves you, not a crown on your head or a leadership position in school. Keeping this attitude before you compete or try out for any team will help you remember your identity.

## 2. You Must Be Gracious

One of the most attractive character qualities is graciousness, especially in the face of failure. Graciousness is when you are kindhearted and courteous no matter what the outcome. Think about this: Whenever a friend beats you in a one-on-one game, how do you respond? Do you run away and pout? Or do you smile, laugh, and congratulate her for winning? As Christians, we are called to be kind and gracious, even when we lose. We need to show Christ's love all the time, even when it is difficult.

### 3. It Is All a Part of God's Will

Whenever you compete for something, you need to give it over to God. Remember that He is in ultimate control. Pray and ask God to help you give that control to Him. He is aware of every little detail in our lives. One verse to remember is Romans 8:28: "We know that all things work together for the good of those who love God: those who are called according to His purpose." God works everything out for good for His children!

### 4. Be Thankful

God calls us to "give thanks in all circumstances" (1 Thessalonians 5:18 NIV). That means thinking positively. Maybe you made some wonderful friends or you became a better teammate or learned something new from a competition. There is always something positive. Focus on those good things and be thankful for them.

### 5. Winning Doesn't Make You a Winner

I remember how after one pageant, we were all very happy for the girl who won, but then we saw her backstage being rude to the staff members. That is not how a winner behaves. A true winner is kind to those around her, puts others before herself, and loves to bring out the best in people. You need to build those qualities in yourself and work every day to put others before yourself. Whether or not you come home with the trophy, your kindness makes you a true winner.

Losing isn't easy, but God uses defeat to strengthen us. It is important to remember 1 Corinthians 9:25: "Everyone who competes in the games goes into strict training. They do it to get a crown that will not last, but we do it to get a crown that will last forever" (NIV). Whenever you compete, keep that verse at the front of your mind. We compete for the Lord.

## What About You?

1. When was the last time you lost at something even after giving it your best (a game, a competition, a tryout)? How did you feel?

2. How do you usually respond when you lose? Do you pout, get angry, or smile and congratulate the winner?

3. Why is it so important for us to be kind and courteous even when we lose?

# You Can Fail Without Being a Failure

### by Pam Gibbs

**Complete this sentence: I am a** __Weirdo__ .

__GIRL!!__

You could have said a gazillion things . . .

I am a girl.

I am a cheerleader.

I am a daughter, sister, friend.

Then you could have added some adjectives . . .

I am a shy girl.

I am a funny girl.

I am a good cheerleader.

I am a great sister. (Yeah, I know, I'm stretching it a bit!)

Sometimes, though, you might define yourself in very different terms. For example, you made a D on your latest spelling test. What if your science fair project bombed? Or you fell while running laps during PE? What then?

I am a __reject__ .

What would you say about yourself?

I am a failure.

Is that what you said? Why?

Unfortunately, many of us would describe ourselves as failures. That's because we have bought into the lie that our worth equals how well we perform. God wants you to know that your worth is not based on how well you do in sports or how funny you are. It is not based on your grades or your communication skills.

God has created you from scratch in His image (Genesis 1:27). You are "fearfully and wonderfully made" (Psalm 139:14 NIV). He created you "for good works, which God prepared ahead of time so that we should walk in them" (Ephesians 2:10). How exciting is that? The problem is, if you see yourself as a failure, you will believe a lie and miss the plan God has for you.

Can you imagine what would happen if a generation of girls began to grasp their worth based on God's Word? If they embraced the truth of being made in God's image? If they sought God and asked Him to show them where He is working so they could join Him there?

What would you do if you weren't afraid of failure?

What would you do if you knew that the outcome wouldn't change your value, worth, or belonging?

Dream. For a minute, just think about what God might want you to do with your gifts and skills and passions and quirks. Then chase that dream. Whatever you think God may have birthed in your heart to do for Him, with Him, and through His strength, go after it. Not to draw attention to yourself or show other people how awesome you are, but to put the spotlight on the One who created you and gifted you. Sing. Speak. Learn. Dance. Share. Jump. Run. Draw. Create. Give. Pray. Go. Try. And keep at it. Don't quit. Keep at it. Winston Churchill once said, "Success is not final, failure is not fatal: it is the courage to continue that counts."

Live courageously. "Be strong and courageous. Do not be afraid; do not be discouraged, for the Lord your God will be with you wherever you go" (Joshua 1:9 NIV). In the end, it doesn't matter whether you succeed or fail. What matters is giving glory to God in whatever you do (1 Corinthians 10:31). With that as your goal, you will never be a failure.

## What About You?

1. Are there things you're afraid to try because you think you might not be very good at them?

2. Why are you scared to fail? What's the worst thing that could happen if you try something new and end up not being very good at it?

3. How can you please God in whatever you do, whether you succeed or fail?

# EPIC FAIL

## by Tami Overhauser

*Though a righteous man falls seven times, he will get up.* —Proverbs 24:16

Have you ever failed at something when you wanted badly to succeed? How did you feel? How did you respond to the failure? Maybe you cried or got frustrated or considered giving up. You may have even felt like your life was ruined. But don't give up just yet! You are not alone! Check out these dream chasers and world changers who failed at first but refused to see themselves as failures.

### Michael Jordan: Basketball Player

After being cut from his high school basketball team, a young Michael Jordan went home and cried in the privacy of his bedroom. But Jordan didn't stop playing, and he didn't let this setback keep him back. He says, "I have failed over and over and over again in my life. And that is why I succeed."

### Babe Ruth: Baseball Player

Before holding his home run record, Babe held a pretty hefty strikeout record! When asked about this, he simply said, "Every strike brings me closer to the next home run."

### J. K. Rowling: Novelist

Before J. K. Rowling became successful, she was fired from a job because she would write stories on her work computer all day long. Luckily, that novel turned into the Harry Potter franchise, which has since made her a millionaire.

## Dr. Seuss: Author

Twenty-seven different publishers rejected his first book. He's now the most popular children's book author ever.

## Walt Disney: Entrepreneur

Before Walt Disney built the empire we see today (Disney World!), a newspaper editor fired him because "he lacked imagination and had no good ideas."

## Albert Einstein: Physicist

We all know Einstein as a genius, but he wasn't known for his intelligence in his early years. He didn't speak until he was four years old and didn't read until he was seven. His teachers labeled him as mentally handicapped, but he later went on to win the Nobel Prize in physics!

## Thomas Edison: Inventor

Thomas Edison failed at least a thousand times before creating the light bulb.

## Abraham Lincoln: Sixteenth U.S. President

Lincoln struggled in the military, failed at starting a business, and lost several runs for public office before becoming president.

## Lady Gaga: Singer/Songwriter

When she was finally signed on to her first major record label, she was fired after only three months.

Don't give up. Don't let one momentary failure define you. Let God teach you, develop you, and help you become everything He created you to be.

My grace is all you need. My power works best in weakness.
—2 Corinthians 12:9 NLT

My flesh and my heart may fail, but God is the strength of my heart and my portion forever.—Psalm 73:26 NASB

Now to Him who is able to do above and beyond all that we ask or think according to the power that works in us.—Ephesians 3:20

Ask and it will be given to you; seek and you will find; knock and the door will be opened to you.—Matthew 7:7 NIV

For I know the plans I have for you, declares the LORD, plans for welfare and not for evil, to give you a future and a hope.—Jeremiah 29:11 ESV

When you fail, how do you recover?

Scan for Video Answers!

# Go Easy on Yourself

## by Meredith Perry

*My outfit doesn't look as cute on me as it does on her. I'm having a bad hair day . . . or bad hair year. I forgot my homework again—why do I always mess things up? Why is it so hard to get along with my friends? I wish I was better at sports. Why does life seem so much easier for everyone else? Why is it so tough to fit in?*

Do thoughts or questions like those ever run through your head? If your answer is yes, you are not alone. From a young age, we girls are especially hard on ourselves. This is often because we feel like we don't measure up to the standards in place around us. We can be self-conscious about our looks, our personalities, and our talents. And those insecurities can get in the way of what God wants to do in and through us.

If you are feeling disappointed in yourself, don't ignore those feelings or pretend they aren't messing with your mind. Face those feelings head-on and deal with them. You were not made to journey through your insecurities alone, so ask a few godly adults you trust to help you figure out who you are and what you are good at. Over time this will help you develop a healthy self-image, and it will deepen your relationships with those adults. Your "self-image" is the picture of how you see yourself.

God's words are even more powerful than people's words. Did you know that our identity is found in Christ? Sometimes that can be difficult to understand when we're feeling really down about ourselves. It can even be hard to believe that it's true. However, God's Word is true even when we don't fully understand it or we don't *feel* like it's true. It can be challenging to see ourselves through God's eyes. In order to do that, we need to learn how to believe the truth of God's Word no matter what our emotions tell us.

Our value is based on who we are, not on what we do right or wrong. God wants us to see ourselves through His eyes. Here's what He says about His children: We are redeemed and forgiven (Colossians 1:14). We are loved (1 John 3:1). We are complete in Christ (Colossians 2:10). We are created in His own image (Genesis 1:27).

It can be easy to get down on ourselves when we make a mistake or have an embarrassing moment. The beautiful part of being Christians is that we all mess up sometimes, but God loves us anyway. No one is perfect, and we're all in need of help. Just because we make mistakes, doesn't mean we *are* mistakes. We all make mistakes, and we all need a Savior . . . a perfect Savior, Jesus Christ. When God looks at His children, He doesn't see our mistakes—He sees Christ inside us, covering all our sins.

In Psalm 139, we are reminded that we're "fearfully and wonderfully made" (v. 14 NIV). The unique qualities and talents He's given us don't make us weird. They make us special and allow us to contribute to the world around us, glorifying God in the individual ways He created us to. When we get down on ourselves, we miss the incredible work Christ has done in and through us as our Savior. Next time you feel less than perfect or wonder if you matter, remember God's incredible love for you! Lift your head up and fix your eyes on Jesus. He has such wonderful plans for you. Don't doubt what He can do through your life!

## What About You?

1. Do you get down on yourself often? What are you hardest on yourself about?

2. Does being hard on yourself help you in any way? Does it make you feel better?

3. Do you believe God loves you and wants to use your life for His purposes? If so, are you willing to repeat that truth every time you start to feel bad about yourself?

# When I Grow Up

## by Vicki Courtney

1. Be Homecoming Queen.

2. Go to college at Duke.

3. Meet Mr. Right.

4. Get married and move into a new house the size of a castle.

5. Become a lawyer.

6. Have first child (boy).

7. Buy a house with a swimming pool.

8. Have second child (girl).

9. Retire at age fifty-five.

10. Live happily ever after.

*H*ave you ever met one of those people who has the next twenty years of life already planned out? She seems to know exactly what she wants to do when she grows up, when she wants to get married, how many kids she will have, where she wants to live, and what sort of house she will live in. I call it living by a checklist.

I'm not much into checklists, but at your age, I was fairly certain that I had it all figured out, at least when it came to a career. I wanted to be a lawyer. In fact, when I got to college, I declared myself a pre-law major. That lasted all of about one semester, so I changed my major to business, then communications, then sociology, then economics. Okay, so maybe I didn't have everything figured out after all.

After five years in college and changing my major five times, I finally graduated with a degree in economics. A career counselor told me that most people with degrees in economics find jobs in banks or someplace where they work with numbers. What? I hate math and working with numbers! Thank goodness I didn't go to work in a bank because I might not have figured out that I was supposed to be a writer all along.

And do you know how I figured out that I was supposed to be a writer? After I was married and had my first child, I began sending out one of those annual Christmas letters every year to my friends and family. I always hated getting Christmas letters from people who had perfect kids and perfect lives. You know, the ones where "Little Johnny just turned one and can sing his ABCs in English, Spanish, and French, blind-folded while tap dancing." The next year the letter brags that he's getting recruitment letters from the ivy-league colleges. They may as well just skip all the bragging and get to the real reason they are sending the letter—it's their fancy way of saying, "We're better than you! Our family is cooler, better-looking, and more successful than yours." So, when I wrote my letter each year, I decided to be honest. One time I even wrote about how my sons had called each other "dummy poop heads" while posing for the Christmas picture that went along with the letter. Another time I wrote about my daughter's habit of tak-ing her clothes off in public places. Don't worry—she was a toddler at the time.

I was honest, and a funny thing hap-pened. Every year when I sent the letter out, my friends and family members told me how they looked forward to my letter because they knew it would make them laugh. Over and over again they told me, "You know, you should think about writ-ing." I didn't take a single writing class in college, and I had never once thought about being a writer when I was your age. And here I am today, a writer. Go figure.

A really good friend of mine said she knew what she wanted to be from the time she was a little girl. She wanted to be a doctor. She graduated in the top of her class, went to college, was accepted into medical school, got mar-ried, and finally realized her dream of becoming a doctor. There was only one problem: when she started her practice, she'd just had her first child. As the days went on, it became harder and harder for her to leave her baby with the nanny so she could have her dream job. She stuck with her "checklist" but was torn.

One day when she came home, the nanny told her not to fix any more bottles for the baby. The nanny had weaned the baby from the bottle and taught him to drink from a cup. That was really tough on my friend because she wanted to be the one to experience her baby's milestones. Then a couple of months later, the nanny told her he had taken his first steps. Once again, my friend had missed it. She told me it was at that point she realized no matter how careful she had been to plan the details of her future, she hadn't figured out how she would make it work once she had children. Today she still practices medicine, but she does it part-time so she doesn't have to miss her kids' big moments. She has other important matters to tend to like soccer games and trips to the park.

My point is this: it's impossible to plan for the future and think about all the details when you don't have all the details yet. If you live your life by a checklist, it allows God little room to direct your steps. There is nothing wrong with having an idea of what you might like your future to be, but don't go overboard by planning it point by point. Besides, God may not agree with everything on your checklist. Or, as my friend

learned, He may add something to the list that is far better than that dream job. Leave room for God to move. There is plenty of time for Him to reveal His plan and purpose for your life. In the meantime, sit back and enjoy the ride.

**We can make our plans, but the LORD determines our steps. Proverbs 16:9 NLT**

## What About You?

1. Have you thought about what you want to be when you grow up? If so, what do you dream of becoming?

2. What are some areas God has gifted you in (for example: sports, academics, art, or music)?

3. Why is it important for us to pray about our dreams and let God lead us to what we will become?

# So, You're Off to Middle School!

## by Vicki Courtney

*I*t was forty years ago, but I remember it like it was yesterday. The first day of middle school. Back in my day we called middle school "junior high," and it only included seventh and eighth grades. Even though it was a long time ago, I remember the mixture of excitement and fear as the first day approached. I carefully laid out my favorite new outfit (hello, this is a very important detail!) and my brand-new Trapper Keeper (ask your mom). I met my best friend in front of the school so we could walk in together and receive our locker assignments. Lockers! How exciting is that?! I could hang up posters of my teen idol crushes and . . . oh no, what if I forgot my locker combination?! What if I didn't get the B lunch period, which was rumored to be the best lunchtime? What if I got the mean science teacher who I heard would make students stand up in front of the class and sing a song if they were caught talking? Ack!

My emotions ping-ponged from excitement . . . to fear . . . to excitement . . . and back to fear.

Can you relate?

The first day of middle school can be exciting.

The first day of middle school can be stressful.

I know starting middle school can be a scary time in a girl's life, so I asked middle and high school girls what piece of advice they would give you about becoming an official middle schooler!

And here is what they said . . .

BYOP (Be Your Own Person)! Nobody else can be you—and you can't be anybody else. Be true to yourself and stick to your morals and values.
— Kensey Rae, 17

Don't get involved in the drama! You are worth so much more than that.
— Kaylin, 14

Don't change your personality in order to hang out with the people considered to be popular.—Ema, 14

Don't let other people's opinion of you dictate what you know to be true about yourself.—Megan, 18

I would tell girls not to take the drama too seriously and to be themselves. Don't change anything to fit in. In high school, you'll look back and laugh at how ridiculous it all seems.—Allison, 15

Try to avoid the girls who love drama.—Caitlin, 13

Be who you really are and don't be fake. Stay away from drama. Don't wear a lot of makeup. You are already pretty the way you are! Keep your locker clean because you have to clear it out in the end! And don't forget to pray!—Jada, 13

Be careful what you tell your friends. Don't share anything you don't want anyone else to know because you can't be sure who will tell your secret. Also, be wise when picking friends. Girls who have drama will have friends with drama!—Caroline, 11

Find a great youth group or a group of friends who will support you, encourage you, and hold you accountable. At school, do your best to stay out of the dating drama because it isn't worth it.—Delaney, 14

Stay more focused on your grades and school than what people think about you. Relax and have fun with your friends.—Macie, 15

Don't worry about boys and dating. You have plenty of time for that later. Don't let others influence your choices. Do what you know is right. Keep your focus on following Christ and having a Christlike attitude and actions.—Megan, 16

Be outgoing, don't be shy. Get to know your teachers because they will help you in the future. Surround yourself with friends who support you and don't expect you to change and become someone you're not.—Aurora, 14

Don't wear name-brand shirts just because everyone else does.—Stephanie, 18

Do your best, don't slack off, and pay attention in class, even if you already know what's being taught. You never know, it may still help you. If someone makes fun of you, don't let it get to you.—Alena, 12

Be yourself. Participate in activities or clubs because you like the activity, not just because all your friends are doing it.—Dailey Rae, 13

Make sure to find the right friends . . . ones who aren't just looking out for themselves or who care mostly about being popular. And don't act like someone you're not just so people will like you.—Olivia, 12

Don't conform. Be who you are. Don't find your identity in guys, clothes, etc. Find your identity in Jesus Christ!—Carleigh, 14

Always be true to yourself! Not everyone will like you, and that's okay. Never try to be someone you're not. Be kind no matter what.—Skyler, 14

# Are You Cell~Mannered?

## by Vicki Courtney

Cell phones. Every family has different rules for when, what kind, or even *if* the kids in the house will get one. You may not have a cell phone of your own right now, but you are probably surrounded by them everywhere you go. Cell phones make it possible to stay in touch with friends and family all the time—which can be good and bad. When people use them properly, phones can make life easier and even more entertaining with all the games and apps. But when people aren't considerate of others when using their phones, it can cause some trouble!

Here are ten rules to help you become a cell-mannered girl:

1. **Turn off your phone in places where you know they're not allowed.** Even if they're allowed, resist the urge to answer if you are in a place where others might consider it rude! (For example, church, weddings, school assemblies, plays, concerts, or movie theaters.)

2. **Never talk while you are in a bathroom.** It doesn't matter if it's your bathroom at home or a public bathroom—don't do it! No one wants to hear a toilet flushing in the background while they're talking to you, nor do people in the bathroom want to hear you talking while they are there too.

3. **Never talk or text when you are having a conversation with others.** If you think the call is important (like, your mom is calling), say, "Excuse me for a minute. I need to get this." Step away and take the call, then apologize when you return. No one likes to be interrupted, so unless it's an important call, it can wait.

4. **Put your phone away while having a meal.** It doesn't matter if you're at home in your kitchen or at a restaurant. The only exception is if you are expecting a call from Mom or Dad or a similar emergency. In that case, excuse yourself from the table to take the call.

5. **Never send pictures or texts from someone else's phone and pretend to be them.** Even if you're just joking around, it can get out of hand and cause a lot of drama.

6. **Do not call or text your friends at inappropriate hours.** Chances are, their parents will eventually find out, and it could give them a bad impression of you.

7. **If your phone has a camera or video feature, never take inappropriate pictures and send them to others.** Never take pictures of strangers, or anyone for that matter, without their permission.

8. **Never talk loudly on your phone or turn the sound up when playing games/apps while you are in enclosed spaces with other people.** (For example, airplanes, cars, elevators, or waiting rooms.) If possible, wait until you are in a bigger space to talk. If you must take or make a call, talk very quietly and keep it brief!

9. **Be sensitive to those around you while using your phone.** Sometimes it's easy to be off in your own little world while talking to someone and forget others are nearby. Don't scream, laugh loudly, or behave in such a manner as to draw attention to yourself.

10. **Follow the rules your parents have given you.** Maybe you only have a cell phone for emergency purposes. You are not alone. That's how most kids start out. It is your job to prove to your parents that you can be trusted with a cell phone. If you follow their rules, you have a better chance of them adding other privileges (such as more minutes or texting) on down the road.

# So Much Pressure!

## by Ali Claxton

We feel the constant pressure to succeed from a very young age. We are always being evaluated and tested by teachers, coaches, bosses, parents, church leaders, and friends. It seems like everyone expects something from us. We feel like we have to be at the top of our game all the time. And it's exhausting!

I teach a group of high school girls at my church. They are smart, funny, and extremely driven. I listen to them talk about standardized tests, honors classes, college prep, service projects, band competitions, sports, auditions . . . and the list goes on. They spend time every day preparing for, participating in, or recovering from some form of intense activity. And they get evaluated on almost everything they do. Life for them often feels like a never-ending series of tests.

It will be a while before you experience the challenges of high school, but even at your age, you probably feel a lot of pressure. Trying to keep up with everyone's expectations can be difficult and frustrating. If you are going to do well and enjoy life, you'll need some help finding balance.

Here are a few tips to help you deal with all that pressure:

## 1. Know your strengths.
It's nice to hear people say, "You can do anything you set your mind to." But just because you *can* do something doesn't mean you *should*. You've been created with unique talents and personality traits. Use those to help you determine what opportunities to pursue. When you focus on activities that come naturally to you, you experience consistent growth and a sense of accomplishment even under pressure.

## 2. Set realistic goals.
Striving for perfection in everything is impossible. A "no mistakes allowed" kind of attitude will lead to a life of unmanageable stress and future health issues. Yes, you should work hard and do your best at all times, but allowing no room for mistakes also leaves no room for growth. Instead of striving for perfection, make it your goal to do your very best. With that perspective, you'll be more willing to try new things and less likely to crack under pressure.

### 3. Focus on what's most important.

We are on this earth to please God. The best way to please God is to love Him with your whole heart and to love other people. Keep that in mind every day, and it will give you peace and joy no matter what you face.

There will always be pressure to succeed. For the rest of your life, you'll be evaluated based on all kinds of expectations. But the pressure doesn't have to crush you. Do your best at whatever you do. And don't lose sight of what matters most.

## What About You?

1. Do you feel pressure to be good at everything you do?

2. What activities do you enjoy? Which activities come naturally to you?

3. How can you please God with your attitude as you participate in activities?

# The Secret to Lasting Happiness

### by Susie Davis

Wouldn't it be great to feel happy all the time?

When I was little, I remember thinking that if I could be happy all the time, my life would be just perfect. In fourth grade I thought that if only I could do a back handspring, I would be happy.

In fifth grade I imagined that getting a lead role in the school play would fill me with happiness. And by sixth grade, I just knew that if one certain boy liked me back, I would be the happiest girl in the whole world.

Even though some of those things did happen to me when I was in grade school, the happy meter in my life didn't always register full. For instance, when I finally found out that one certain boy liked me back (which I begged God for and told Him it would make me oh-so happy forever!), it didn't mean that I stayed happy. Boys are fun, of course, but you won't wake up every day saying, "Oh my goodness! I am the luckiest person alive because a boy likes me! I'm really happy, and I'll be happy forever!" No, that's kind of crazy, and you probably realize that. But I wonder . . . do you know what will make you truly happy every day?

Try something. Write down ten things that you believe will make you happy on the list below. Start each with, "I would be happy if . . . "

1.

2.

3.

4.

5.

6.

7.

8.

9.

10.

Now look over the list and ask yourself honestly: *are those the things that will keep me happy forever?* There's nothing wrong with wishing a certain boy will like you or hoping your parents will break down and get you a cell phone with unlimited texting, but so many of our "happy" wishes are about believing that certain things or situations can make us deep-down happy, when that's something only God can do.

There is only one way to get deep-down happy that lasts and lasts. It's something God gives, and it's called *joy*. Joy is a deep-down happy from God. And joy is what will help you feel happy even when you don't have all you want or things aren't going your way.

See, the world's version of "happy" comes and goes. It can fly away if you lose your tablet or if your mom doesn't let you go to a birthday party. But joy is different. It's a feeling of happy that no one can take away from you. Even if you lose your prized possession and your mom is driving you crazy, you can still feel the kind of joy that God gives. Romans 15:13 says it this way: "May the God of hope fill you with all joy and peace as you trust in him so that you may overflow with hope by the power of the Holy Spirit" (NIV).

This verse promises that God fills us with joy when we trust Him. Trusting God is the key to having a happy, joyful heart.

*Joy* is your way of remembering that God is in control of everything in your life!

It works something like this: Let's say you lose your tablet. You've looked for it everywhere for over a week, and it's nowhere to be found. Joy can be found when you stop beating yourself up for losing it, thank God for the time you had it, and realize that you can still enjoy your life without it. While it's a big bummer to lose something you like that much, you can still laugh and play and thank God for your life. That's joy because it's your little way of trusting in God. It's your way of remembering that God is in control of everything in your life, whether or not you have a tablet.

When we trust God and believe that He has a good plan for our lives, we experience the deep-down, God-given happy called joy. Does that mean that we will never feel disappointed? No, of course not. We will all have our share of sad times in life—that happens. But we don't have to let the sadness take over our lives. We can trust God instead.

Jesus even told us that we would have disappointments. In John 16:33, He said, "Here on earth you will have many trials and sorrows. But take heart, because I have overcome the world" (NLT).

The truth is, there will be unhappy stuff that happens, and sadness will come into our lives; but God has promised to take care of us if we trust Him. So my happy wish for you and for me is to hand over our hearts to God and let Him fill them up with His kind of happy—the happy that lasts and lasts: joy!

## What About You?

1. Why does our happiness come and go from day-to-day?

2. What is joy? How is it different from happiness?

3. How does trusting God and having joy impact our sense of peace and self-worth?

# Think This, Not That

by Tami Overhauser

Do you ever worry about not being good enough? Never fear: God has great plans for you! His Word is a constant reminder that His plans are good and He has gifted you to shine for His glory. In the moments when you feel like you don't measure up, think about these words:

"For I know the plans I have for you," declares the LORD, "plans to prosper you and not to harm you, plans to give you hope and a future."—Jeremiah 29:11 NIV

I am able to do all things through Him who strengthens me.
—Philippians 4:13

Trust in the LORD with all your heart, and do not rely on your own understanding.—Proverbs 3:5

So do not throw away your confidence; it will be richly rewarded.—Hebrews 10:35 NIV

Be strong and courageous! Do not be afraid or discouraged. For the LORD your God is with you wherever you go.
—Joshua 1:9 NLT

Commit everything you do to the LORD. Trust him, and he will help you.—Psalm 37:5 NLT

And whatever you do, in word or deed, do everything in the name of the Lord Jesus, giving thanks to God the Father through him.
—Colossians 3:17 ESV

# Get More
# LIKES

# The Cross or the Crowd?

### by Vicki Courtney

When my daughter was in second grade, she was chosen to perform on a high-level cheer team for a spring show. Most of the girls on the team were in middle and high school, so I worried she might see and hear some things that didn't line up with her faith in God. Sure enough, she came home one day very upset about some words in the song her cheer coach had chosen for the performance. "Mommy, it says something very, very bad. God wouldn't like it one bit." *Yikes*, I thought. She was so upset by the words in the song that it took me a while to convince her it was okay to even whisper the words in my ear. Finally, she leaned over and whispered, "The song says, 'Oh, my God.'"

While that may not seem like a big deal, my daughter had been taught (by her parents and at church) that it is not right to use the Lord's name in vain. She knew that the song didn't use God's name in a respectful way. In fact, it was disrespectful. She loved God so much that it troubled her heart to hear the phrase because she knew it dishonored God. I was proud of my daughter, be- cause she was more concerned with showing God the respect He deserves than fitting in with the crowd. It would have been easier for her to say nothing. I knew that it would be harder and harder for her to stand up for her faith as she got older and many of her Christian friends were following the crowd.

Most of us want to fit in. It's only a matter of time before you will be faced with a choice to "fit in" or "stand strong." First Corinthians 16:13 says, "Be on your guard; stand firm in the faith; be courageous; be strong" (NIV). Standing strong may come with a price. Choosing the cross (the Christian faith) may mean you are not accepted by the crowd. Nothing in this world is more important than your faith. I love how the verse above says to "be courageous." It takes more courage to follow the cross than it does to follow the crowd. Following the crowd is easy. It's the popular path.

As you get older, you will be exposed to many situations when you will have to decide whether to follow the cross or the crowd. Such as:

- Lying

- Cheating

- Bullying

- Gossiping

- Using the Lord's name in vain

- Dressing inappropriately

- Cheerleading or dance-team moves that are suggestive

- Sex outside of marriage

- Same-sex relationships

- Experimenting with drugs and alcohol

- Looking at inappropriate things on the Internet

Many of your friends will think these things are okay. Sadly, even some of your friends who say they are Christians will choose to follow the crowd rather than the cross. It might be easy right now to follow the cross, but it won't always be easy. In fact, it may get harder and harder as time goes on to stand firm in the Christian faith. That's why it's important to decide today who you will follow when faced with a choice. The crowd . . . or the cross? Which one will it be?

## What About You?

1. Can you think of a time when you had to decide whether you would follow the crowd or the cross?

2. Is it hard for you to "be courageous" and follow the cross?

3. What are some ways you can "be on your guard" and "stand firm in the faith"?

# QUIZ

## Are You Following the Right Crowd?

Birds of a feather flock together. Have you ever heard that saying before? It kind of sounds like something you might read in Proverbs, but it really just means people who think and act alike are drawn to the same kind of people. Proverbs talks a lot about making wise choices and staying on the right path. So it's time to figure out if you are "flocking" with people who are on a path to wisdom or you're "flocking" with people who are headed for folly (foolishness)! Take this quiz to find out.

Answer these questions based on the group of girls you currently hang around. How would they likely act in these sticky situations?

1. After a long week at school, your mom drops you off at a movie to meet some of your friends. You had your mom's approval to see the newest PG, tween movie. Also, your best friend's big sister who's in college is going to sit with your group. When you greet your friends at the ticket counter, they . . .
A. buy tickets for a completely different movie with a PG-13 rating you know your mom would not approve of.
B. follow through with the original plan and buy tickets for the PG movie your mom approved.

2. It's time for gym class, and your teacher makes you a team captain for kickball. As you take turns picking members, your first pick is a girl who usually doesn't get picked until last. Your friends . . .
A. stare at you like, *Why on earth did you pick her and not me?*
B. smile and nod at your sweet example of loving others.

3. You are at Olivia's house for her birthday sleepover. She has invited one of her cousins, who no one really knows. Her cousin is a little odd and sometimes says strange things. When she leaves the room the first time, your friends . . .

A. immediately look at each other and start to giggle, laugh, and say how weird she is.

B. act as if nothing is different.

4. It's fourth-period English class, and you totally forgot to study for a quiz. Your friends are sitting near you in class and see the panic on your face. In the middle of the quiz, the teacher leaves the room. Your friends . . .

A. immediately look your way to mouth you the answers.

B. keep to themselves and catch up with you after class to ask how you did.

5. While browsing your favorite store at the local mall with one of your friends, you see some really cool hair clips that are too expensive for you. Your friend suggests . . .

A. you just sneak them in your purse.

B. you ask the clerk if they can hold them for a few days. Then ask your mom if you can earn some money by doing chores.

**6.** Your older sister bought the coolest new shirt last weekend. You borrow it for the end-of-the-year school party, and accidentally spill red punch all over it. Your friends tell you to . . .

A. just put the shirt back in her closet, and she'll never know. The next time she wears it, she'll think she stained it.

B. tell your sister you're sorry. Offer to help clean it or replace it with babysitting money you earned.

**7.** You and your friends are invited to Tessa's sleepover party on Friday. She's a sweet girl, and you all accepted her invitation. The next day Emma also invites you and your best friend to her sleepover on Friday. Emma is the coolest girl in the grade *above* yours. Your best friend suggests you go . . .

A. to Emma's house and tell Tessa something came up. Surely she'll understand.

B. to Tessa's since you had already committed to her, and thank Emma for the invitation.

**8.** Your group is given an opportunity to take part in a service project on a Saturday helping less-fortunate people. Your group of friends . . .

A. goes but gripes about having to be there and looks for ways to kill time by taking looooong bathroom breaks.

B. goes and enjoys the experience serving together.

# How Did You Score?

### Caution: Danger Ahead! (five or more A's)

Stop. Do not pass go, do not collect $200. You are not following the right crowd! You choose friends who lead you down the wrong path. Remove yourself from groups of friends who pressure you to compromise your values or base their opinion of you on whether you will follow them on the path to foolishness. True friendships will encourage you to seek God and make the right choices. Proverbs 17:17 says, "A friend loves at all times" (NIV). Keep this in mind when you find yourself with the wrong crowd and their actions don't look very loving!

### Stuck at the Fork in the Road (equal number of A's and B's)

You seem to hang with friends on both paths. It might be time to take a closer look at the group that encourages you to make bad choices. Are they really worth it? While it's always good to be a light to those girls, make sure your closest friends are on the right path.

### On the Straight and Narrow (five or more B's)

You are on the right path! You see the value of choosing friends who are like-minded and do not compromise your values. These friends will encourage you to do what is right.

# Do You Have the "If~Only" Disease?

## by Vicki Courtney

One time, when I was speaking to a group of women, I asked them this question: "If you could be any person in the world, who would you want to be?" I could tell they were thinking about it because of the looks on their faces. After a few minutes, I told them that I had brought a picture of who I would want to be.

I asked for a few volunteers to come up and take a peek at the picture in the frame to see if I had picked the same person they had. One by one, they came up and looked at the picture. One by one, they quickly shook their heads.

When the women returned to their seats, I turned the frame around for everyone in the audience to see. It was a mirror!

When I look in the mirror, who do I see? Me! I was showing them that if I could choose to be anyone in the world, I would choose to be me! I felt sad that when the other women looked into the mirror, they said they would not have chosen to be themselves.

If you could choose to be anyone in the world, who would you want to be?

Would you want to be yourself? You may have said yes right away, but I bet there have been times you have wanted to be like someone else. Maybe someone you watch on TV? Or maybe that pretty girl in school? Or maybe the one who always gets picked first in gym? We have all compared ourselves to someone else and wished for a minute that we were that person.

I'm going to let you in on a little secret: many of us moms deal with this same issue. I call it the "if only" disease. You know, it's the disease that makes you say to yourself, *If only I had her (fill in the blank).* Her cute personality. Her money. Her hair. Clothes. Friends. Talent. Grades. Boyfriend.

Don't worry—there's a cure for the "if only" disease. Focus on being happy with how God has created you and what God has given you. This cure isn't easy to follow, especially if your best friend just won the award you worked hard for! But with a little practice, you will be thanking God instead of complaining to Him.

Here's an example: if you are envious of a friend's stuff, remember this verse: "For where your treasure is, there your heart will be also" (Matthew 6:21).

In other words, if we think too much about the things we have (treasure), our hearts and thoughts will constantly focus on those things instead of on what really matters—God. It's okay to have things we treasure, but we shouldn't be too focused on them.

Sometimes I find myself wishing I looked like someone else or had someone else's money, talent, or stuff. When I realize I'm catching the "if only" disease, I stop and say thank You to God for what I do have. If you begin to thank God for His blessings instead of complaining to Him (or your mom!), before long you will discover that the "if only" disease has been cured.

God made you to be special, just the way you are. He gave you your own look, your own talents, your own everything! No one else on earth is like you.

## What About You?

1. If you could be anyone in the world, would you choose you? Why or why not?

2. What are you thankful for right now (such as your family, health, or talents)?

3. What is one thing you can do to fight the "if only" disease the next time it hits you?

# Wise Words from High School Girls

*W*hat advice or words of wisdom would you give tween girls when it comes to caring too much about what others think?

## Sam, 14

I would say that basing your worth in God is important. If you go into each day with the mind-set that God, not the mean girl in your class, defines who you are, you'll begin to notice a difference.

## Mittie, 14

I used to struggle with peer approval, but I switched my focus to being the best I could be, being nice to everyone, and simply being who I am. We all will have people in our life who will not like us or get annoyed with us, and that is okay. I encourage girls to talk to someone (like a mentor or your parents) to let them know you are struggling.

### Caroline, 15

I struggled with caring way too much about what others think of me. I constantly tried to get others' approval by having cuter clothes or better grades. What others thought of me controlled so much of what I did. Then God showed me that I do not need the approval of others to feel good about myself. My clothes and my grades do not matter to Him, and I always try to remind myself that He will love me no matter what.

### Erin, 18

Peer approval will never satisfy like you think it will. EVER. More times than not, people are not thinking about you nearly as much as you think they are. The most beautiful thing any girl or any person can be is completely themselves. God crafted us so specifically that when we are able to be ourselves, people see that beauty. From my personal experience, when you are confident in your flaws, quirks, and all-around who God made you to be, people respond better than if you try to fit some mold. Don't seek the hollow, ever-changing approval of peers. This type of approval will always be hollow, always be unfulfilling, and always be something that you're chasing instead of achieving. Focus on living as God would desire.

# QUIZ

## Are You a Copycat?
### by Susie Davis

There's nothing more frustrating than a friend who copies everything you do! And although that is totally irritating, sometimes we can fall into the trap of being copycats ourselves. Take this quick quiz to see if you are a COPYCAT!

**1. One of your friends comes to school, and you just love the new jeans she is wearing. You . . .**

A. compliment her and go on your way.

B. ignore the fact that she has new jeans because you're jealous.

C. ask her where she got them—so you can get a pair just like them.

**2. A teammate decided to get bangs cut for the first time. She asked everyone she knew if she should try it, and she finally got up the courage to do it. You . . .**

A. tell her the bangs look great and give her a hug.

B. act like you didn't notice she got new bangs.

C. say, "Well, it's about time!" and then go home, get out a pair of scissors, and cut your own bangs.

**3. You and a bunch of your friends are going out to eat. You're all sitting at the table ready to order. You . . .**

A. look over the menu quickly, pick out what you want, and tell the waiter as soon as he pulls out his pad and pen.

B. order what you think you want but then change your mind after a few of your friends order—worried you might not have ordered the best thing.

C. tell the waiter you want to go last so you can figure out which food item is the most popular with your friends. Then once they all order, you place yours, which is the same as theirs.

**4. Your mom decided you need some new clothes because you've grown so much this year. You . . .**

A. make a plan to go out shopping with your mom at the stores she chooses.

B. throw a fit and tell her it's too boring and stressful to go shopping with her.

C. take a poll at school, asking all your friends where they buy their clothes, then hand the list to your mom, telling her that the only way you'll go shopping is to go to the stores where your friends buy their clothes.

**5. This summer your parents planned for you to go to an overnight camp for the first time. You . . .**

A. get online with your parents and go to the camp website. You look at all the photos of the camp and print a copy of the "what to bring" list so you can start getting ready.

B. roll your eyes and tell them that camp is not your thing.

C. anxiously grab the phone and start calling every friend you know to see if they can talk their parents into letting them go to camp with you.

**6. Your parents decide that your family will start going to church every Sunday. You . . .**

A. tell them you are excited about the idea of meeting new friends who believe in God.

B. warn them that you really have no desire to get up early on Sundays and go to church.

C. tell your parents you'll only go where your friends go, so they should probably start calling your friends' parents.

# How Did You Do?

**Mostly A's.** You're the DAWG! You can make decisions by yourself and stand on your own, which allows you to experience all life has for you! You have strong confidence in the marvelous way God made you. Way to go!

**Mostly B's.** Okay—so you could use an adjustment in your attitude about new things and standing alone. Life is full of great surprises, and the truth is, you're missing out by not being more open-minded. In addition, your ungrateful attitude is likely to make people dislike being around you. Try to be more flexible and positive!

**Mostly C's.** Meow! You're a COPYCAT! Your decisions are ruled by what others think of you. Although it is important to enjoy your friends, you are too controlled by what they think and do. Why not pray for courage to make some good decisions all by yourself? You should decide for yourself what you will wear to school or which camp to go to this summer. You were created by God, and He thinks you are fabulously made—and that includes *your* ideas about what *you* think is pretty, delicious, fun, or cool. Celebrate the unique you!

# Talk About Embarrassing!

## by Vicki Courtney

We've all had them happen. No one can escape embarrassing moments. True, some are more embarrassing than others, but everyone has a story about a heart-beating, palm-sweating, cheeks-blushing moment when time stood still and you wanted to curl up and die.

I had an incredibly embarrassing moment happen at a big event where there were lots and lots of Christian authors and singers. I had my teenage daughter with me, and we'd heard that Mandisa was going to be there signing her new CD. We had just finished eating dinner and were leaving a restaurant with some friends when someone in our group pointed to a lady and said, "Hey look, isn't that Mandisa over there?" She was walking out of the restaurant in front of us. Being the awesome mom that I am, I thought it would be a good idea to catch up with her and get her autograph for my daughter. We were only about fifteen feet behind her and I started yelling, "Mandisa!" No answer. "Mandisa!" Still no answer. "Mandisa!" By this time, I had caught up with her. I tapped her on the shoulder and said, "Mandisa,

my daughter and I just love your music and would love to get your autograph."

I'm not usually one to get starstruck, but I couldn't help noticing how beautiful she was in person. She smiled and very graciously said, "I would love to give you my autograph, but there's only one problem. I'm not Mandisa." Now, of course, this probably explains why she never turned around when I was screaming someone else's name. I can't remember exactly what I said to her, but I know my face was beet red. I apologized and walked back over to my daughter and my friends, who were laughing their heads off. I'm talking laugh-so-hard-you-almost-wet-your-pants kind of laughing. While they tried to catch their breath from laughing, I wanted to crawl into a little hole somewhere and never come out.

We may not be able to control those unexpected embarrassing moments, but we can choose how we react to them. In the situation above, I had two choices: (1) I could dwell on it for the rest of the day and beat myself up for being such a dork, or (2) I could laugh my head off and move on with life.

I chose to laugh about it, and now when I think about that embarrassing moment, I crack up. Of course, my daughter never stopped cracking up. She still reminds me about it to this day! And get this: I told the girls in my office about it when I got back, and one of them got me Mandisa's new book and signed her name on the front and left it on my desk. The note said: "Vicki, it was so great meeting you! Mandisa." When I saw that, I just had to laugh at myself over the whole thing.

The truth is, while a moment may be extremely embarrassing, no one will really dwell on it as much as you. Within minutes, it is usually forgotten. Learn a lesson from me—embarrassing moments are just part of life, and you never outgrow them. Oh, and one more word of advice. You might not want to chase down people for their autographs unless you're absolutely sure of who they are!

## What About You?

1. Do you embarrass easily? When was the last time you got embarrassed?

2. Are you able to laugh at yourself and move on, or do you let embarrassing moments ruin your day?

3. Why is it important to learn how to brush things off and not get upset when things happen and make us look silly?

# Don't Make a Fool of Yourself!

### by Vicki Courtney

*Desire without knowledge is not good—how much more will hasty feet miss the way! A person's own folly leads to their ruin, yet their heart rages against the L*ORD.*
—Proverbs 19:2–3 NIV*

Raise your hand if you've ever done something really stupid as a result of not taking some time to think it through.

I'm guessing that most of us have our hands up right now, and if you don't, it's just a matter of time.

I remember a guy in my fourth-grade homeroom class who did something really, really stupid because he didn't take a minute to think about what he was doing. We were having the end-of-the-year class party, and our home-room mom brought snacks and drinks for the class. The drinks were ice-cold Cokes—the kind in the glass bottles! The boy picked up a bottle, took a few sips, and then said, "Hey, watch this." He then proceeded to put his index finger into the bottle opening to see if it would fit. It fit, all right—so tightly that he couldn't get his finger out! He tugged and tugged, but it didn't help. His finger was a perfect fit in the bottle!

He was too embarrassed to tell our teacher, so he walked around with a Coke bottle dangling off his finger for the next hour or so. After a while his finger began to turn different colors, and he figured he better do something about it. He finally told the teacher, and she sent him to the nurse's office. I don't know what kind of magic the nurse did to free his finger from the Coke bottle, but he came back to class about a half-hour later with the color back in his finger and a little extra color in his cheeks. How embarrassing!

Proverbs 19 reminds us of the importance of thinking things through, rather than making decisions on the spur of the moment. As you get older, you are going to face many important choices, and you will either respond with wisdom (good judgment) or folly. Folly is basically foolish behavior. Proverbs 19:3 reminds us, "A person's own folly leads to their ruin, yet their heart rages against the Lord" (NIV). Some people will actually make poor choices and then turn around and blame God for the results!

God wants to be a part of your everyday life. He wants to walk by your side and help guide you to make wise choices. Like, for example, not putting your finger into a Coke bottle to see if it fits. Cokes were made for drinking, not wearing, right?!

Proverbs 19:8 (NIV) offers this advice: "The one who gets wisdom loves life; the one who cherishes understanding will soon prosper."

## What About You?

1. Have you ever done something really foolish? Describe the situation.

2. What might keep you from doing foolish things in the future?

3. Why does God want us to have a wise heart and make good decisions?

# What's Your Reputation?

## by Vicki Courtney

*Choose a good reputation over great riches; being held in high esteem is better than silver or gold.*
—Proverbs 22:1 NLT

When I was in second grade, my homeroom teacher held a contest at the end-of-the-year party. She brought a giant, monster-size jar of gumballs and placed it on her desk. She then handed us each a slip of paper and told us to estimate how many gumballs were in the jar and write it down. The person whose number came the closest to the actual number of gumballs would get to take home the whole jar as a prize. She gave us a few minutes to study the jar, and no one made a sound. I mean, we're talking about a summer-long supply of gumballs—who doesn't want to win that, right?

Finally I came up with a number and wrote it down on my slip of paper. The teacher gathered them up and then announced the number of gumballs. Unfortunately I didn't win, but my best friend did! Of course, that meant that I was sure to get my hands on some of those gumballs over the summer, so I was happy for her. We would just have to figure out a good hiding place for the jar so her pesky little brother wouldn't find it!

My friend won the jar of gumballs because her estimated number came closest to the actual number of gumballs in the jar. You've probably learned to estimate numbers in math class, but did you know that it's also possible to "estimate" people? For example, if I call out the names of a few of the most popular Disney Channel celebrities and ask you to think of two or three words to describe each person's character, you could probably come up with words pretty quickly. And the words you think of would help estimate that character's "reputation."

I'm not sure if the word *reputation* has appeared on your list of spelling words yet, but it's a word that every young person needs to know. The dictionary defines *reputation* as the "accepted estimation of someone." Basically everyone has a reputation. For example, I had a friend in third grade who loved to play board games whenever I went over to her house. However, there was one little problem: whenever she saw that she might lose the game, she would quit and say she wanted to do something else. It drove me crazy! After a while, I got tired of it and quit going over to her house. When my mom asked me why I didn't want to go, I told her that she didn't play fair and it wasn't fun anymore. She found new friends to invite over, but it was only a matter of time before they, too, began to complain about her being a sore loser.

She got a reputation for not playing fair, and as a result, she had a hard time making and keeping friends. Eventually no one wanted to go to her house because it was such a frustrating experience. How sad that in the end, she cared more about losing a silly board game than losing her friends!

Our reputation is important because it represents who we are and what we stand for to the world around us. When we live our lives to please God and love others, our reputation will be one that attracts people and makes them want to hang out with us. Ultimately, our reputation is another way we can point others to Christ.

Be mindful of the reputation you have among your friends and classmates. Do what you can to protect it so that others will think about Christ every time your name crosses their minds.

## What About You?

1. Does it matter to you what other people think about you?

2. What kind of reputation do you have right now? What do people think about when your name comes up?

3. If you are not happy with your reputation, what can you do to change it?

How would you like other people to describe you?

Scan for Video Answers!

# Bullying Survival Tips

by Rachel Prochnow

A small blonde girl stands in the middle of the cafeteria clutching her food tray. Her eyes scan the room: Groups of kids are at each table. She searches for someone she can call a friend. Nervously, she heads toward the table with the group of girls she has known for years. Right when she puts her tray down, the other girls immediately stand up and walk away—leaving her completely alone at the table. Devastated, tears well up in the girl's eyes as she runs to the bathroom.

Have you ever been bullied? Has someone ever said something mean about you? Or has a friend said something hurtful to you? The story of the small blonde girl was actually about me. Throughout middle school and the beginning of high school, I was bullied by my classmates. I remember feeling completely alone. I remember feeling that I had no friends. There are a few things I wish someone would have told me when I was being bullied, and I want to share those with you.

## 1. You Are Not Alone

God promises never to leave you or forsake you (Deuteronomy 31:6). Even when it feels like you have no one, you always have your Father in heaven. He loves you so much. Never forget His promise to be with you through everything, especially the difficult times.

## 2. You Are a Daughter of the King

Don't lose sight of your identity. You are a daughter of the Most High. You are a princess, and God is watching over you. I always remember Luke 12:6–7: "Are not five sparrows sold for two pennies? Yet not one of them is forgotten by God. Indeed, the very hairs of your head are all numbered. Don't be afraid; you are worth more than many sparrows" (NIV). God cares about every tiny detail. He is watching over you, and He cares what you are going through.

## 3. Tell an Adult

If you are being bullied, you should tell an adult you trust, like your mom or a youth leader. They might be able to fix the problem and help you through the situation. They can also lead you in prayer. God puts certain people in your life to guide you. It helps tremendously if you have an adult who has been there before walking you through it.

## 4. Be Kind

The best way to deal with a bully is to be kind to him or her. The Bible commands us in Proverbs 25:21–22, "If your enemy is hungry, give him food to eat; if he is thirsty, give him water to drink. In doing this, you will heap burning coals on his head, and the LORD will reward you" (NIV). Be kind to those who are not kind to you. When someone says something mean to you, respond out of kindness. The Bible tells us in Proverbs 15:1, "A gentle answer turns away wrath, but a harsh word stirs up anger" (NIV). Sometimes a kind word and a loving response can change someone's heart. When I was in middle school, a girl wrote a mean poem about me. It really hurt my feelings. Instead of getting angry, I took her aside and asked her why she would write something so mean about me and if I had done anything to hurt her feelings in the past. My kind response to her meanness took her completely by surprise. She ended up apologizing, and the bullying stopped after I approached her in love.

If you are being bullied, don't lose sight of who you are. You are a daughter of the Creator of the universe.

Remember that God is watching over you and loves you immeasurably. Make sure to talk to an adult you trust and who loves you. They will able to help you through the difficult time. Try to respond out of love and kindness. Show the bully Christ's love. Remember that when someone bullies, it is normally because they are insecure about who they are and want to put others down. Their negative view of themselves makes them feel the need to belittle those around them. God can change people's hearts, and He can use you to show others His love. The bullies need Christ's love too.

## What About You?

1. Have you ever experienced some form of bullying?

2. How did you respond?

3. How does knowing that God loves you help you face times when people are mean to you?

4. If you are still experiencing bullying, have you asked an adult for help? Who can you talk with today?

# QUIZ *Are You a Bully?*

## by Rachel Prochnow

It's hard to be kind and compassionate to others all the time. We should always consider how our words and actions affect those around us. They have power— they can cut deep, and they can heal. Take this quiz to see how you would react in different circumstances, and find out if you behave like a bully.

**1. There's a new girl in your class. One of your friends starts making fun of her glasses. What do you do?**

a. Tell your friend to stop making fun of her and introduce yourself to the new girl.

b. Join in with your friend. You're just glad she's not making fun of you!

c. Stay quiet. You feel bad that the new girl is being made fun of and you don't want to join in, but it's really not any of your business.

**2. Your best friend, Amanda, is in a different class this year, and she starts to become friends with a new girl. How do you respond?**

a. You spread a lie about her new friend. If Amanda thinks badly of her new friend, maybe she won't want to hang out with her anymore and you'll have your best friend back.

b. Call Amanda and see if you can hang out with her and her new friend. If Amanda likes her, she's a friend worth meeting!

c. Start spending time with another girl in your class.

3. **You start a Bible study for the girls in your class, but you are frustrated that some of the girls aren't really taking it seriously. What do you do?**

a. You privately ask one of your friends why she thinks some of the girls aren't taking it seriously. You ask her if she has ideas on how you can improve the study.

b. At the next Bible study, you call out everyone who didn't do the reading and make them feel bad about it.

c. You call off the Bible study. You are so discouraged that you don't think it's worth doing it anymore.

4. **There's a big reading competition at school, and you really want to win. You spend every spare moment you have reading nonstop. Finally, the big day arrives, and another girl reads one more book than you and comes in first. What do you do?**

a. You ask to speak to your teacher in private and tell her that you think the other girl cheated and didn't actually read all those books.

b. You tell the girl congratulations and that you were impressed by how many books she read. But once you walk away from her, you start telling people how you think you deserved it more.

c. You're impressed that she read that many books! You tell her congratulations and ask her if she has any good book suggestions for you.

5. **Your sister gets a beautiful new necklace for her birthday. It's the same one you have been wanting, and you are so sad that she got it instead of you! How do you respond?**

a. Decide to be happy for her! When you see her wearing it, you tell her how beautiful it looks on her.

b. Ask to speak to your sister in private, and try to convince her that it's not as pretty as she thinks it is. Maybe you can get her to trade it for an old, ugly necklace of yours.

c. Remain upset and pouty that she got it instead of you. Then you run away to your room so people will wonder where you are and you will be the one to get attention.

6. There's a new boy in your class, and he doesn't know anyone. You go and introduce yourself to him and become friends. A few weeks later, one of your friends sees you talking to him at recess and starts telling everyone he has a crush on you. You are so embarrassed. What do you do?

a. Laugh it off and tell your friends he only thinks of you as a friend. Tell them you are happy that he transferred to your school.

b. Rather than stick up for him, you tell your friends later that it's probably true, even though you know he just wants to be friends.

c. You ignore it and walk off. It is so humiliating, and you just want to get away from the situation.

7. Your cousins are in town for the week, and your grandma puts out a board game for you and your cousins to play. You hate losing, and it looks like your cousin is beating you! What do you do?

a. You remember that it is just a game, and you try your best to remain positive!

b. You stop playing in the middle of the game. If you're not going to win, it's not even worth playing.

c. Start muttering rude comments to your cousin. If she beats you, she's not going to be happy about it.

8. There is a new girl at your school, and all the boys are talking about how pretty she is. It is so annoying to you and your friends. How do you treat her?

a. Tell her to her face that she isn't as big of a deal as everyone thinks she is. Better to put her in her place before she gets a big head.

b. Get jealous and start spreading rumors about her behind her back. It's not fair that she is getting all this attention.

c. Reach out to her and see if she wants to hang out. Even if all the boys like her, she still needs a friend.

*Now add up your points with the following chart, according to what responses you chose!*

**Question 1**
a: 1 point
b: 3 points
c: 2 points

**Question 2**
a: 3 points
b: 1 point
c: 2 points

**Question 3**
a: 1 point
b: 3 points
c: 2 points

**Question 4**
a: 3 points
b: 2 points
c: 1 point

**Question 5**
a: 1 point
b: 3 points
c: 2 points

**Question 6**
a: 1 point
b: 3 points
c: 2 points

**Question 7**
a: 1 point
b: 3 points
c: 2 points

**Question 8**
a: 3 points
b: 2 points
c: 1 point

**8-12 points: You are not a bully!** You know that your words and actions have power, and you use them to build others up and make them feel accepted and loved. This is great because as Christians, we always want to show others their value in Christ and make them feel important and cared for. Way to go!

**13-19 points: Somewhere in the middle.** Sometimes you stand up for what is right, and sometimes you go with the crowd. Remember that Christ calls us to stand up for what is right, even when it is difficult! Make it a point to show others God's love and make them feel loved and accepted.

**20-24 points: Bully alert!** Instead of responding out of anger or jealousy, try to respond out of kindness and love. Try to see the good in others and celebrate with them when they succeed. Remember John 15:12: "My command is this: Love each other as I have loved you" (NIV). Love others as Christ has loved you!

# More Than a Number

by Rachel Prochnow

The two friends analyzed the picture, brows bent together in concentration.

"But do you think it's Instagram worthy?" asked the taller of the two. Her small, brunette friend grabbed her iPhone and held it close to her eyes, scrutinizing every detail.

"Yeah, for sure. Your hair looks awesome. Plus, that app we found makes your skin look flawless. You will definitely get at least a hundred likes." Triumphant, the willowy blonde hit Share.

The next hour was riddled with worried glances at her phone. She bit her lip, having only gotten twenty-four likes in forty-five minutes—an awful like-to-minute ratio. She turned to her friend. "Should I take it down?" she asked. "I've barely gotten any likes. How many people have already seen it? Do you think people will notice if I take it down at this point?" Her friend fell silent, a sympathetic look crossing her face.

You might not have a cell phone or social media apps yet, but you probably have friends or older siblings who do. Whatever the case, it is important for you to know that your worth is not about how popular you are on social media. We have the need to feel loved, to feel accepted. Deep within our souls, we long to be accepted. We want to be liked, and that longing is normal. Who doesn't want to feel loved or cared about?

The rise of social media has made us all highly aware of just of how popular we are among our peers. The number of likes you get on a picture, the number of followers you have on Instagram, or the number of views you get on your Snapchat story have enabled us to equate our popularity with a number under a picture. I know I've struggled with this.

The scene I described above is pretty much a conversation I've had with my friends countless times. It's only been over the past year that I've realized that the number of likes I get or the number of followers I have does not determine my worth. In fact, it has zero connection with my worth.

My worth is found in Christ.
Your worth is found in Christ.
He *never* changes.
He *never* gives up on you.

Isn't that truth so much better than finding your value in the hands of your peers, whose likes and dislikes change on a daily basis?

We all need to be accepted. The need is rooted deep within us. It comes from our need for Christ. Our souls long for completion through a personal relationship with Him. It's not really the number of likes you get that you want. What you truly want is to be accepted and loved no matter what. That type of love and acceptance can only come from having a relationship with the Creator of the universe, who loves you regardless of your popularity on earth.

Whenever I struggle with my identity, I always recall 1 John 3:1: "See what

great love the Father has lavished on us, that we should be called children of God! And that is what we are!" (NIV).

We are children of God. Just let that sink in for a second.

When you walk around with that kind of power at the front of your mind, does it really matter what other people think of you?

Jesus Christ died for you. When you are armed with that truth, you can have a healthy view of social media and popularity.

Social media can be a really good thing. It's fun to share exciting things happening in your life with your friends. But it can be a bad thing when it controls what you do, or when you constantly check your phone to monitor the number of likes you receive. If you have a phone and are on social media, I challenge you to examine your relationship with it. Does it determine what you do? Do you find your identity with who likes your picture? Or how many likes you get?

Instead of being focused on your social media accounts, dig into the Word of God. Grow into your identity as the daughter of the Most High. Spend time praying and drawing near to Him. He promises, "You will seek me and find me when you seek me with all your heart" (Jeremiah 29:13 NIV). Find a good book that challenges you as a Christian. Understand that your worth comes from Him and Him alone.

# What About You?

1. Do you have social media apps or know people who do?

2. What do you think is good about social media? How can it become a bad thing?

3. Why is it so important for you to see your value based on God's Word instead of other people's opinions of you?

# NEVER EVERS

NEVER EVER find your identity in how many likes you get or how many followers you have.

NEVER EVER put social media before Christ.

NEVER EVER compare number of likes with friends.

NEVER EVER post pictures or messages that compromise your values or identity in Christ.

NEVER EVER forget that you are representing Christ.

# Dressed to Impress

## by Vicki Courtney

Have you ever been fishing? My youngest son is crazy about fishing. We have a lake house, and he will often set his alarm for early in the morning and head out on a kayak with his fishing gear in hopes of catching a gigantic catfish or largemouth bass. Fortunately, my son is only interested in the challenge of catching the fish; and once he does, he pulls out the hook and throws it right back in for a second chance. (That's your cue to say, "Awww, poor little fishies.")

Some days my son catches a bunch of fish, and other days he catches nothing. He tells me it's all about the lure he uses on the end of his fishing line. You've seen lures before—they come in all shapes and sizes. Most are shiny and shimmery so the fish will be drawn to them when they see them in the water. Fish wouldn't be interested in a plain ol' hook, now would they? No!

Believe it or not, sometimes the clothes girls wear can act as a lure. Some clothes can catch the attention of others, but not in a good way. Dressing to lure means dressing to attract the wrong kind of attention. I'm talking about really tight shirts, short shorts and short skirts, and low-cut jeans that show some skin. Maybe you've seen girls at your school dressed this way. Or maybe you've seen older girls on television dressed this way. I'm pretty sure you have because it's hard to escape them. They are everywhere!

As you get older and your body changes, you will realize that there are a lot of fashions sold in stores that could act as a lure: clothes that attract the wrong kind of attention. To be clear, I'm not talking about clothes that are fun styles or bright colors. I'm talking about clothes that God would not approve of or want you to wear. Sadly, a lot of girls don't realize that what they wear can be a reflection of who they are on the inside.

When you believe in Jesus Christ, the Holy Spirit comes to live in your heart and you are supposed to be a light for Christ. You know the song, "This little light of mine, I'm gonna let it shine"? Well, when you dress to lure, you draw the attention away from God and put it on yourself. Matthew 5:16 says, "In the same way, let your light shine before others, that they may see your good deeds and glorify your Father in heaven" (NIV).

Christian girls should dress to be pure. Dressing to be pure means wearing clothes that God would approve. In 1 Corinthians 6:19–20, God tells us that our bodies are not our own: we were bought at a price, and therefore, we should honor God with our bodies. Dressing to be pure shows that you feel good enough about yourself and don't need to "lure" the wrong kind of attention. A good exercise to try is what I call a "mirror check." A mirror check is when you stand in front of a mirror each morning and say, "Would Jesus want me to wear this outfit?" That is one of the ways we can honor God with our bodies, as the Bible verses above encouraged us to do.

I know it may be hard to see all the fashions and want to fit in with some of the other girls who are wearing clothes that "lure." I am not saying you can't be in style. It is possible to dress in a way that is both fashionable and pure, but it will take extra time and patience to find clothes that will pass the mirror test. As a homework assignment (don't worry—you won't be graded!), you might want to take a look in your closet to make sure your clothes say "pure" instead of "lure." If they say "lure," it might be time to go "fishing" for a new wardrobe!

## What About You?

1. What do your clothes say about you?

2. Would the outfits you have worn this week pass the "mirror test"? If not, are you willing to put those clothes aside and begin dressing differently?

3. Why is it important to honor God with the way we dress?

# Why Doesn't He Notice Me?

## by Kat Williamson

Certain words bring up strong emotions, such as *pop quiz* (fear), *dessert* (joy), or *funeral* (sadness). One word in particular has brought on a lot of different emotions throughout my life: *boy*. In elementary school, I didn't care much about boys, but everything changed in sixth grade when I developed my first crush. At that point, the word *boy* brought forth excitement, but since then, that same word has also caused feelings of insecurity and hurt. There have been many times when I felt strongly for a boy who didn't return my feelings or even notice me at all. All too often in those early years, I based my self-worth on relationships with boys; and when they didn't work out, it crushed me.

So, are all relationships bad? No! Is it okay to want boys to notice you? Yes! God created guys and girls uniquely and with purpose. It's natural to find boys interesting and attractive as we get older. However, boys shouldn't be our primary focus. When we only strive to gain the attention of boys, we become focused on their opinions of us. In other words, when all our efforts go toward trying to get boys to like us, we give them a lot of power to either make or break our self-worth—and that isn't fair to us or to them!

Instead, our focus should be on Jesus Christ. Hebrews 12:2 tells us to fix "our eyes on Jesus, the pioneer and perfecter of faith. For the joy set before him he endured the cross, scorning its shame, and sat down at the right hand of the throne of God" (NIV). What does it mean to "fix our eyes" on Jesus? It means to focus on serving Him, loving Him, and making His name known. When we're focused on Jesus, we put Him above all others in our lives. With all of the distractions that the world has to offer, it can seem impossible to completely fix our eyes on God; but as we focus more and more on Him, we begin to base our worth on how He see us—as His precious, beloved daughters. When our identities are firmly rooted in Christ, we'll eventually attract boys who are also pursuing Christ and who will treat us with respect and honor.

Maybe you're starting to see boys in a new light. You notice the interesting and unique ways that God has created them, and that intrigues you. Or maybe you only see boys as friends right now. Either way, that is okay—everyone matures at different speeds, and there is no need to rush into this phase of life. You have plenty of time to figure all this out. But regardless of the feelings that come forth when you talk about boys, the most important thing to remember is to keep your eyes fixed on God—not on boys, not on others, not on yourself—only on Him. As you focus on knowing Him more and serving Him with your life, He will lead you to the places and the people (and yes, maybe even the boy) that He desires for you.

## What About You?

1. What do you think about boys at this point in your life?

2. Do you like getting attention from boys? Why or why not?

3. Do you let whether or not a boy notices you affect how you feel about yourself? In what ways?

# Idols in Your Life

## by Susie Davis

"Do you have what it takes to become the next American Idol?" The familiar words echoed through the family room as my daughters turned up the volume, preparing to watch *American Idol*. It was one of the programs on TV that my whole family enjoyed together. We listened and laughed and tried to guess who would make it through to the next round. As the weeks passed, we watched with excitement, wondering (and a few of my family members voting!) who would become the next American Idol.

It was an interesting and entertaining show. But have you ever really thought about what the word *idol* means? In this case, the show revolved around everyone trying to become the idol. It was the goal to achieve. To become the idol meant that everyone thought you were fabulous! Instantly popular. Instantly on the cover of every magazine. And instantly winning a recording contract. In the Bible, God talks a lot about idols, and it's not at all like the show.

In Leviticus 26:1, God says, "Do not make idols or set up carved images, or sacred pillars, or sculptured stones in your land so you may worship them. I am the LORD your God" (NLT). God is commanding the people not to make idols. In those days it wasn't unusual for someone to grab a stone, carve it, and set it up as something to be worshipped or adored. I know it sounds pretty silly, but that was the custom back then, and

> Do not make idols or set up carved images, or sacred pillars, or sculptured stones in your land so you may worship them. I am the LORD your God.
> —Leviticus 26:1 NLT

> *Don't let your heart be deceived so that you turn away from the LORD and serve and worship other gods.*
> *—Deuteronomy 11:16 NLT*

God didn't like it. The reason He didn't like it is because He wanted to be worshipped and adored. God stills wants to be worshipped as first place in our life all the time—just as He did with the people in the Old Testament. So He addressed the problem of idolatry throughout the Old and New Testaments.

Deuteronomy 11:16 says, "Don't let your heart be deceived so that you turn away from the LORD and serve and worship other gods" (NLT). The gods in this case were the carved stones: anything other than the Lord God. And though it is unbelievable to think of worshipping a stone carved by a man and making a god out of it, the truth is, we have a tendency to make idols out of things these days too.

Just think about it. Look at your life to see if you might be worshipping some things or activities more than you worship God. I don't mean that how you spend most of your time is necessarily a signal of what you care about most, because you spend the majority of your day sleeping or going to school. No, what I am asking is: What takes first place in your heart most often? Then ask yourself if that thing takes a higher place in your life than God.

It could be a sports activity. Or a hobby. Maybe even a friend or a family member. Maybe being popular is your god or idol. Or looking perfectly beautiful is what you spend all your time thinking about and trying to make happen. It can really be just about anything at all, and when it becomes an idol in your life, you can tell because nothing else matters except the thing that is getting your whole focus. It can be a good thing (like a family member) or a not-so-good thing (like trying to be perfectly beautiful all the time), but whatever it is, you know it's an idol when God gets shoved out of your life.

I remember a time in my life when I idolized boys and having a boyfriend. I thought about it all the time, and at school, boys were my whole focus. I thought about days as good or bad depending on whether or not I was able to talk to the boy I liked at school. If things were going well with a boy I liked, I was happy. If things weren't going well,

I was sad. The boys in my life had control over my happiness (though luckily they didn't know it!) because I worshipped them. And while there is nothing at all wrong with being attracted to the boys in your life—it's actually quite normal—I was putting far too much focus on them. They were a good thing in my life that turned into a bad thing because of idolatry. In this case, boys took first place, and God tumbled to second or third. Not a good thing.

God doesn't want our whole focus to be on other people and things. He wants our love and attention. The Lord God wants first place in our lives, and as our Maker, He knows what is best for us. He loves us with an everlasting love, and He doesn't like to see us loving things more than we love Him. When that happens, our lives turn upside down. We become more and more focused on things other than God, and they end up controlling our lives and breaking our hearts.

## What About You?

1. Are there idols in your life right now? What are they?

2. Will you pray and ask God for help with the problem of idols in your life?

3. Will you allow God to be first place in your life?

# Dear Daughter,

When you were small, you loved Dr. Seuss. We read his books all the time: *One Fish Two Fish Red Fish Blue Fish*, *The Lorax*, *The Cat in the Hat*, *Green Eggs and Ham*, and even a short poem he wrote called "Happy Birthday to You!"

You liked Dr. Seuss books because they rhymed and made funny sounds. Sneetches and Sylvester McMonkey McBean. Cindy Lou Who and the Grinch. Benjamin B. Bicklebaum. And who could forget Sam-I-Am? Fun names. Colorful pictures. Crazy, made-up worlds. You loved his imaginary worlds. I loved his books for a different reason—because of the lessons they taught.

One of your favorite lines from Seuss's birthday poem was this:

> "Today you are You,
>    that is truer than true.
>       There is no one alive
>          who is Youer than You."

Some days I see that confidence in you. Other days I don't. You come home worried about something a girl said about you, worried that she might not like you anymore.

Believe it or not, it's normal to wonder whether somebody likes you, especially at your age. And it's even normal to wonder what other people think of you. But I don't ever want you to let others' opinions be the boss.

As a tween, you believe that everyone has an opinion about you. You worry that they'll see the pimple that popped up overnight. You worry that they won't like your outfit. You wonder if they think you have cool friends or lame parents (no, I'm not lame!). I get it. I was your age once. I remember that feeling. I can still remember feeling embarrassed if I did something stupid, like the time I was in the church van and threw up all over the most popular kid in school, who just happened to be sitting in the seat in front of me. (Yes, that really happened!)

Can I let you in on a little secret? Everyone else is worried about the same things you're worried about. When that popular girl walks into the cafeteria, she's wondering what *you* think about her. You may wonder if people are thinking about you, but other kids are really thinking about what *you* think about *them*. I'm beginning to sound like Dr. Seuss, aren't I?

A woman named Eleanor Roosevelt made a great statement once. She said, "You wouldn't worry so much about what others think of you if you realized how seldom they do."

Every girl your age and every boy your age worries about what others think of them.

Here's the problem: How do you decide whose opinion matters the most? Who is right? Is it the popular crowd? Or is it other smart kids like you? What about your best friend? She might think you're great. But what if she gets mad at you for some reason and decides you're not cool anymore? Does that mean you're not cool? What people think about you will change. And different people will have different opinions of you. So which one is right?

Seriously, who is right?

You are.

And what God says about you is true (I'll write you another letter about that later). I want you to put this on your bulletin board: What you think of yourself is more important than what people think of you. If you think you are creative and funny and silly and smart (and you are), then does it matter what other people think? Nobody gets to tell you how to feel about yourself—unless you let them.

When I was your age, I missed out on a lot of fun things because I was afraid of what my friends would think. I didn't try out for band because it wasn't cool. I didn't tell my friends about how much Jesus loved them because I worried they would think I was too religious. I didn't go to some of the school activities because I didn't want to be alone and look like a dork. I missed out because I let other people determine my worth.

As you grow up, you'll have to decide every day how to be yourself when other people want you to be different—funny, skinny, smart, cool, rebellious, angry, talkative, withdrawn. My prayer is that you'll decide to believe what God thinks about you. He created you uniquely to be you—not somebody else.

And if you do—if you decide for yourself who you want to be and where you want to go—then cool things will happen.

Love, Mom

# Don't Be in Such a Hurry to Grow Up

## by Kat Williamson

I once heard a fable about a magic spool of thread, which, when pulled, would fast-forward one's life. As the story goes, a little boy received the spool after wishing he could skip his childhood and become a grown-up. Throughout his life, he would pull the thread every time things were hard or life seemed mundane. At the end of the story, the boy had become an old man; and as he thought back over his life, he realized how short his time on earth had been. He came to understand (a little too late) that every season of life is a gift, even the hard, boring, or frustrating seasons.

Although this fable is just a silly story, the little boy's desire to be older sadly reflects the way a lot of people look at life. Maybe you, too, struggle to enjoy the age you are right now. It's easy to feel envious of the freedom that high school students, college students, and adults have. But this stage of life is a beautiful gift. Why? Well, because God has a purpose for it.

Think about it: God could have created humans to be fully grown adults at birth, but He didn't. He created infancy, childhood, and adolescence, and He has a purpose for every life stage. Right now you have responsibilities associated with schoolwork, sports, or music practice, but you probably don't have to worry about paying your own bills, working at a job, or taking care of a family. He gave you a childhood so that you could experience the simple joys of youth and innocence. While in this stage of life, you'll grow to know God more and better understand who you are in Him—and that, my friend, is a gift!

Whenever I struggle with finding contentment (peace and joy) in my stage of life, I like to read through Ecclesiastes 3:1–12. This passage begins with the words, "There is an occasion for everything, and a time for every activity under heaven" (v. 1). It then lists out the different occasions that we will face while on earth (vv. 2–8). Some of those occasions sound good (a time for birth, a time to laugh, a time to dance), while others sound less pleasant (a time to die, a time to weep, a time for war); but it's important to remember that He's given us a purpose in every stage of life. Verses 11–12 do a good job of summarizing how we should respond in such occasions: "He has made everything appropriate in its time. He has also put eternity in their hearts, but man cannot discover the work God has done from beginning to end. I know that there is nothing better for them than to rejoice and enjoy the good life."

Did you catch that? We're called to rejoice through all stages of life—even when it looks more fun and glamorous to be older or more mature. Those verses remind us that God is in control of our time here on earth; we are not. We can rejoice in the knowledge that God has us exactly where He wants us right now.

## What About You?

1. Are you enjoying where you are in life right now, or do you wish you were older?

2. Why do you think it's hard to be content (joyful) in every stage of life?

3. What are some things you are thankful for that are part of your life right now?

What do you love about your age right now?

Scan for Video Answers!

# Think This, Not That

## by Tami Overhauser

Relationships can be difficult. Fortunately, God has given us some guidelines when it comes to managing our friendships. We don't have to fall into the trap of caring too much about what other people think of us.

Don't be selfish; don't try to impress others. Be humble, thinking of others as better than yourselves. –Philippians 2:3 NLT

Let the words of my mouth and the meditation of my heart be acceptable in your sight, O Lord, my rock and my redeemer.–Psalm 19:14 ESV

Search me, God, and know my heart; test me and know my anxious thoughts.–Psalm 139:23 NIV

Accept one another, then, just as Christ accepted you, in order to bring praise to God. –Romans 15:7 NIV

Pay careful attention to your own work, for then you will get the satisfaction of a job well done, and you won't need to compare yourself to anyone else.–Galatians 6:4 NLT

A friend loves at all times.–Proverbs 17:17 NIV

You have heard that it was said, "Love your neighbor and hate your enemy." But I tell you, love your enemies and pray for those who persecute you. –Matthew 5:43-44 NIV

If it is possible, as far as it depends on you, live at peace with everyone.–Romans 12:18 NIV

Treat people the same way you want them to treat you.–Matthew 7:12 NASB

# The TRUTH of the Matter

# Worth Far Above Rubies

## by Vicki Courtney

*Who can find a capable wife? She is far more precious than jewels.*
—Proverbs 31:10

*She draws on her strength and reveals that her arms are strong.*
—Proverbs 31:17

*She sees that her profits are good, and her lamp never goes out at night.*
—Proverbs 31:18

*Her hands reach out to the poor, and she extends her hands to the needy.*
—Proverbs 31:20

*Strength and honor are her clothing, and she can laugh at the time to come.*
—Proverbs 31:25

*She opens her mouth with wisdom and loving instruction is on her tongue.*
—Proverbs 31:26

*Charm is deceptive and beauty is fleeting, but a woman who fears the* Lord *will be praised.*
—Proverbs 31:30

You may not have had the word *virtuous* on your list of spelling words yet, but if you had grown up a hundred years ago, chances are you would know exactly what the word meant. In fact, teenage girls from a century ago often wrote in their diaries about their desire to become "virtuous" women. Proverbs 31 is a passage that is known by many women of all ages. It gives a list of qualities that make up a virtuous woman. Back in biblical times, mothers would often help their sons memorize verses 10–31, so they would know what qualities to look for when looking for a virtuous wife someday.

Today *virtuous* is not a word you hear mentioned often. But that doesn't mean that it's not still important to become virtuous. So what does it mean? If you look *virtuous* up in the dictionary, you might find words like *good*, *moral*, and *pure*. Those can be hard words to live up to, which is why Proverbs 31:10 tells us that a virtuous wife is "more precious than rubies." If you find a virtuous woman, she is like a rare and priceless gem or a sparkling jewel. It's one of the most important Bible passages for a girl to know.

Let's see if you can match up the following verses that describe a virtuous woman with words that mean the *opposite*. Draw a line to connect them.

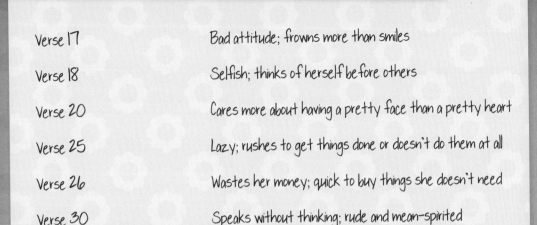

| Verse 17 | Bad attitude; frowns more than smiles |
| Verse 18 | Selfish; thinks of herself before others |
| Verse 20 | Cares more about having a pretty face than a pretty heart |
| Verse 25 | Lazy; rushes to get things done or doesn't do them at all |
| Verse 26 | Wastes her money; quick to buy things she doesn't need |
| Verse 30 | Speaks without thinking; rude and mean-spirited |

My favorite verse in the Proverbs 31 passage is verse 30 because it contains the most important quality: fearing the Lord. This describes a woman who loves Jesus more than anything or anyone else in the entire world. She lives to please God more than people. If you aim to live up to that verse, the qualities that are listed in the other verses will most likely follow. Girls who love Jesus more than anything usually care about the poor, work hard, speak with wisdom and kindness, and spend their money wisely.

So, what do you say? Do you want to grow up to become the kind of woman who is like a rare and priceless jewel? Becoming a virtuous woman is worth the hard work and effort. The first step on your list: fall madly in love with Jesus!

## What About You?

1. Can you think of someone you know who is a "virtuous woman"? If so, who is it?

2. Even though we don't hear much about being "virtuous" in today's world, do you think it's still important to God?

3. Reread verse 30. What do you think it means when it says, "Charm is deceptive and beauty is fleeting"?

4. Do you think most women spend more energy and time on being beautiful on the outside or beautiful on the inside? Which one do you think God cares more about?

# Oh, Just Thinking About You

## by Vicki Courtney

> For it was You who created my inward parts; You knit me together in my mother's womb.
>
> I will praise You because I have been remarkably and wonderfully made.
>
> Your works are wonderful, and I know this very well.
>
> My bones were not hidden from You when I was made in secret, when I was formed in the depths of the earth.
>
> Your eyes saw me when I was formless; all my days were written in Your book and planned before a single one of them began.
>
> God, how difficult Your thoughts are for me to comprehend; how vast their sum is!
>
> If I counted them, they would outnumber the grains of sand; when I wake up, I am still with You.—Psalm 139:13–18

I've always been amazed by verse 18 in Psalm 139 that says God's thoughts about us outnumber the grains of sand. Have you ever walked along a sandy beach? If you've ever taken a minute to scoop up a handful of sand and sift it through your fingers, you know it would be impossible to count how many grains of sand are contained in that one handful.

One science writer, David Blatner, wrote a book called *Spectrums*. He set out to calculate an approximate number of grains of sand contained in the whole world. (Talk about a hard job!)

He began by calculating how many grains are in a teaspoon and then multiplied that number by the mass (an estimated measurement) of all the beaches and deserts in the world. He discovered that the earth has roughly (*very* roughly) $7.5 \times 10^{18}$ grains of sand, or seven quintillion, five hundred quadrillion grains.[*]

Or if you were to write that number out, it would be about 7,500,000,000,000,000,000 grains of sand on earth!

---

[*] David Blatner, *Spectrums* (New York: Walker & Company, 2012).

Chances are, you didn't even know there was such a number as quintillion. Most of us have heard of a million or a billion, but a quintillion is impossible to even understand. Look at it this way: if you counted one number every second of the day and night, it would take you approximately 316,889,554 years to count to one quintillion.

But that's only counting to *one* quintillion. God's thoughts are probably way past even seven quintillion! That would take about 221,822,687,800 years; and last time I checked, no one has *ever* lived that long. So, yeah. Take that off your bucket list.

The next time you find yourself worrying about what others think, remember this number: seven quintillion. Then smile, and know that you are greatly loved by the God of this universe.

## What About You?

1. How do you feel when you think about God's great love for you?

2. What does His love tell you about your worth as a person?

3. Do you live with the confidence of one who is infinitely loved by God, or do you let the opinions of others make you question your worth? Explain.

What does God think about you?

Scan for Video Answers!

# Who Do You Think You Are?

### by Ali Claxton

We all want to believe we have value, that we add something beautiful to this world. We want to wake up with confidence and walk through our days unhindered by labels and insecurities. We want to feel brave and extraordinary.

We want our lives to matter. But if we're being honest, most days we don't *feel* all that significant. We're unsure of ourselves more often than we care to admit. We can't see past our mistakes and weaknesses to the potential planted deep inside us.

The struggle to find our true identity is a necessary part of life's journey. Where you choose to search for your sense of self-worth will make all the difference. You won't discover your infinite value in temporary things like appearance, achievements, or other people's opinions. There is only one source that can show you who you are and who you're becoming. The only way to truly see yourself is to look through the lens of the One who created you.

And here's what He says about you . . .

## You are beautiful:

*I will praise You because I have been remarkably and wonderfully made. Your works are wonderful, and I know this very well.*
*—Psalm 139:14*

**You are alive and free:**

But God, who is rich in mercy, because of His great love that He had for us, made us alive with the Messiah even though we were dead in trespasses. You are saved by grace!
—Ephesians 2:4–5

Therefore, if the Son sets you free, you really will be free.
—John 8:36

**You are a new creation:**

Therefore, if anyone is in Christ, he is a new creation; old things have passed away, and look, new things have come.
—2 Corinthians 5:17

**You are a child of God:**
See what great love the Father has lavished on us, that we should be called children of God! And that is what we are!
—1 John 3:1 NIV

**You are victorious:**
You are from God, little children, and you have conquered them, because the One who is in you is greater than the one who is in the world.
—1 John 4:4

**You are forgiven:**

He has not dealt with us as our sins deserve or repaid us according to our offenses. For as high as the heavens are above the earth, so great is His faithful love toward those who fear Him. As far as the east is from the west, so far has He removed our transgressions from us. As a father has compassion on his children, so the LORD has compassion on those who fear Him.

—Psalm 103:10–13


Therefore, no condemnation now exists for those in Christ Jesus, because the Spirit's law of life in Christ Jesus has set you free from the law of sin and of death.

—Romans 8:1–2

**You are a friend of God:**

*I do not call you slaves anymore, because a slave doesn't know what his master is doing. I have called you friends, because I have made known to you everything I have heard from My Father.*
*—John 15:15*

**You are a child of light:**

*You are all children of the light and children of the day. We do not belong to the night or to the darkness.*
*—1 Thessalonians 5:5 NIV*

**You are a citizen of heaven:**

*But our citizenship is in heaven, from which we also eagerly wait for a Savior, the Lord Jesus Christ.*
*—Philippians 3:20*

**You are an ambassador for Christ:**

*Therefore, we are ambassadors for Christ, certain that God is appealing through us. We plead on Christ's behalf, "Be reconciled to God."*
—*2 Corinthians 5:20*

God's Word paints a beautiful picture of your identity. His truth defines you. Let His words sink deep into your heart and give you the confidence to be who you are.

## What About You?

1. If someone asked you to share who you are, how would you describe yourself?

2. Which of the verses above is your favorite? Why?

3. Do you ever think about the way God's Word describes you? How do these truths give you comfort and joy?

4. How can knowing who you are in Christ help you in every area of your life?

# Walking Like a Princess

## by Rachel Prochnow

What do you think of when you hear the word *princess*? Do you think of a huge castle with servants? Do you think of a prince who sweeps the princess off her feet and rescues her from an evil dragon? What I am about to tell you might shock you. Are you ready for it? You are a princess! Once you accept Christ as your Lord and Savior, you are now a daughter of the King of kings.

Let that sink in for a second.

Now comes the big question: How should a princess act? What should a princess do? The princesses in Europe have years and years of lessons to know exactly how to act in different circumstances. But what do you do? You haven't taken etiquette lessons or studied how a princess should act. As a fellow princess and daughter of the Lord, I want to share some tips that I have learned about how a princess should carry herself.

## 1. Her Heart Belongs to the Lord

As a daughter of God, your identity is rooted in Him. Therefore, your focus and heart ought to belong to Him. Seek Him every day. Spend time in prayer, read His Word, and draw near to Him. Your heart should strive to become more and more Christlike every day. Your goal is to honor and bring glory to your heavenly Father.

## 2. She Is Humble

A true princess recognizes that she did nothing to earn the title of *princess*: it was given to her as a gift. She remembers that and walks in humility and thankfulness every day. Matthew 5:5 says, "Blessed are the meek, for they will inherit the earth" (NIV). A princess realizes that she has been blessed and has a humble and thankful heart.

## 3. She Sees the Good in Others

A princess is able to recognize that everyone has been "fearfully and wonderfully made" (Psalm 139:14 NIV). When she interacts with others, she notices the good qualities that God has blessed them with and celebrates those gifts. She is happy when her friends do well and cheers them on when they succeed.

She does not get jealous, but instead she loves them and celebrates their successes.

## 4. She Is a Peacemaker

She is happiest when there is peace and unity among her friends. She does not gossip or spread rumors about anyone. Instead, she brings people together and always tries to make sure everyone feels loved and included. Matthew 5:9 states, "Blessed are the peacemakers, for they will be called children of God" (NIV). She always looks for a way to bring in someone who might not have friends.

## 5. She Is Kind

A princess is kind even when it is hard. Even when someone is mean to her, she responds out of love and kindness. Proverbs 15:1 says, "A gentle answer turns away wrath" (NIV). She is kind to everyone and looks for ways to serve those around her and make their lives better.

## 6. She Puts Others First

Even though she is a princess, she puts the needs of others before her own. She sees the example that Christ set by washing His disciples' feet (John 13:10), and she wants to imitate (copy) Christ. She always looks for ways to lift others up and help them. She remembers

Philippians 2:3–4: "Do nothing out of selfish ambition or vain conceit. Rather, in humility value others above yourselves, not looking to your own interests but each of you to the interests of the others" (NIV).

Always walk in the power and confidence of your identity as a daughter of the King of the universe. Remember that you are representing Christ and try to imitate Him through serving, loving, and showing His love to everyone you meet. Remember, a princess always points to the King she belongs to!

## What About You?

1. Do you think of yourself as a princess? Why or why not?

2. Are you a humble and thankful princess or one who thinks of yourself first? Explain.

3. How can you use your words and actions to point others to King Jesus?

# QUIZ

## What Kind of Princess Are You?

### by Rachel Prochnow

God has blessed each of us with gifts and talents—we all contribute to His kingdom in a unique and beautiful way! Have you been wondering how God has gifted you? Take this quiz to better understand how your talents can make a huge impact in the kingdom of God!

1. **One of your friends is getting ready for a class project, and she has to get up in front of the class. You can tell she is really nervous because she hates speaking in front of people. What do you do?**

   a. You run to the vending machine, get her a Twix bar because it's her favorite, and leave it on her desk with an encouraging note about how you know she will do an awesome job.

   b. You offer to stay after class and help her with some techniques you learned from your last presentation; you talk her through the parts she is the most nervous about.

   c. You tell her that you are going to pray for her, and you spend the next week praying every day that God would give her courage.

2. **You are at a birthday party, and you notice your friend's little sister is all alone. No one is talking to her, and she looks sad because she's the youngest one at the party. What do you do?**

   a. You run up to her and encourage her to get involved with the volleyball game everyone is about to play. She's worried that she might not be good because she so much smaller than everyone else, but you encourage her to play anyway.

b. You go talk to her and ask her how her school year is going. You listen to her and make suggestions on how her school year can be the best one yet. You were just there two years ago!

c. You ask her what is wrong, and she tells you that she is actually sad because her dog is sick. You ask her if it's okay if you pray with her right now for her dog to get better.

3. Your best friend's project got picked for the final round of the science fair. She really, really wants to get first place, and the student body is going to vote next week. What do you do?

a. You clap and cheer the loudest when her name is announced as a finalist in the school assembly. You immediately run up and hug her after the assembly and tell her you know her project will win.

b. After the assembly you congratulate her and tell her you will spread the word to the students in your class to vote for her project next week.

c. You remind her of Luke 1:37, which says, "With God nothing will be impossible" (NKJV). You tell her you will pray for her every night.

4. You go into the bathroom during lunch and see the new girl in your class crying because she hasn't made any friends yet. What do you do?

a. You put your arm around her and encourage her that it just takes time to adjust to a new school. You tell her you will be her friend and that she should eat lunch with you and your friends.

b. You go up to talk to her, and you notice she is super shy. You tell her you used to be the same way the year before, but you learned to face your fear and talk to some of the other girls. You invite her to sit with your friends, and you introduce her to each one.

c. You ask her what is wrong and invite her to have lunch with you and your friends. Later that night at bedtime, you remember to pray for her.

5. You are walking down the hallway, and you overhear one of your friends fighting with her mom. Her mom wants her to stay home this weekend and help her get ready for her grandparents' upcoming visit. What do you do?

a. You encourage her to make the right decision and listen to her mom. You tell her that next weekend you can all get together instead of this weekend.

b. You offer to help her and her mom get ready for the weekend! You know doing things together is much more fun than doing it on your own!

c. You sympathize with her and remind her of Colossians 3:23: "Whatever you do, do it heartily, as to the Lord and not to men" (NKJV).

6. Every fall you and your friends try out for the track team. Everyone made it except one of your friends. What do you do?

a. You encourage her to try out again next year and remind her that it won't come between your friendship.

b. You get together with her and think of other activities she can get involved in. You encourage her to give something else a try.

c. You remind her that God is in control. You take a few minutes to pray with her and ask God to comfort her heart.

## Mostly A's

*Princess Encourager:* You understand that your words have power, and you always think of ways to encourage your friends to be the best versions of themselves! You are a considerate child of God and always look for ways to build others up—whether it's a kind word or a sweet note.

## Mostly B's

*Princess Problem Solver:* If one of your friends is a having an issue, you are the one to find a solution! You are active and engaging when it comes to solving issues. You find solutions to problems your friends are facing.

## Mostly C's

*Princess Prayer Warrior:* You understand the power of prayer and Scripture! You always lend a prayerful heart to others and offer encouragement through the Word of God. You seek ways to pray for those around you, and you always point them to God.

# Wise Words from High School Girls

W hat is a favorite Bible verse that has helped you get through your school years and the pressures you face?

## Sam, 14

"Therefore, I urge you, brothers and sisters, in view of God's mercy, to offer your bodies as a living sacrifice, holy and pleasing to God—this is your true and proper worship. Do not conform to the pattern of this world, but be transformed by the renewing of your mind. Then you will be able to test and approve what God's will is—his good, pleasing and perfect will" (Romans 12:1-2 NIV).

## Rylie, 18

The Bible verse that has most helped me when I've struggled is Psalm 139:13-14: "For you created my inmost being; you knit me together in my mother's womb. I praise you because I am fearfully and wonderfully made; your works are wonderful, I know that full well" (NIV). I read it every day. Whether the day was good or bad, I read and remembered that God made me perfect in His image. Every single attribute and characteristic God has given me was completely thought out by Him. Don't question why you are one thing and not the other; instead, be grateful in knowing that God has blessed you tremendously and will use you in wonderful ways.

## Mittie, 14

"Have I not commanded you? Be strong and courageous. Do not be afraid; do not be discouraged, for the LORD your God will be with you wherever you go" (Joshua 1:9 NIV).

## Caroline, 15

One of my favorite Bible verses is Isaiah 41:10, which says, "So do not fear, for I am with you; do not be dismayed, for I am your God. I will strengthen you and help you; I will uphold you with my righteous right hand" (NIV).

## Tate, 14

"Am I now trying to win the approval of human beings, or of God? Or am I trying to please people? If I were still trying to please people, I would not be a servant of Christ" (Galatians 1:10 NIV).

"Blessed is she who has believed that the Lord would fulfill his promises to her!" (Luke 1:45 NIV).

### Erin, 18

I don't have a specific verse. My recommendation would be to find a daily devotional, get a journal, and write down your prayers and verses you come across on any given day in your life. Different verses speak to you at different times.

### Alle, 18

My favorite verse would have to be Jeremiah 29:11: "'For I know the plans I have for you,' declares the LORD, 'plans to prosper you and not to harm you, plans to give you hope and a future'" (NIV). This verse always gave me hope in knowing that I am never alone in my hardships, no matter what the case. God is always there and feels all of the pain and excitement that I experience each and every day. Even if it feels like no one is there to walk through your struggles or excitements, know God is with you always wherever you go.

# Congratulations, You're an Heir!

## by Vicki Courtney

It's the kind of news story that leaves you shaking your head in confusion. On December 17, 2012, the body of Timothy Henry Gray, age sixty, was found under the overpass of Union Pacific Railroad in Evanston, Wyoming. According to a coroner's report, the police found no signs of foul play and determined the cause of death was hypothermia (too cold).

But Gray wasn't your average homeless person. He was the adopted great-grandson of former US senator William Andrews Clark and the half great-nephew of the reclusive New York copper heiress Huguette Clark, who had died the year before at the age of 104 with an amassed $300 million fortune. Gray was among twenty great-nieces and great-nephews who each stood to inherit $19 million from their great-aunt's estate. Attorneys for the relatives had been searching for Gray in the weeks before his death. Not that the fortune would have likely made much difference. Family members had not seen Gray in more than two decades, claiming he had severe post-traumatic stress symptoms due to childhood traumas. A coroner reported that at the time of his death, a wallet was found on him, and it contained undeposited checks from a few years back, one of which was described as "large."

Timothy Gray's story is a desperately sad account about an adopted heir to a great fortune who never realized his true worth. Instead, he chose to live as a homeless person. You might be surprised to find we share something in common with Gray's story. We, too, are adopted heirs to a great fortune.

But when the set time had fully come, God sent his Son, born of a woman, born under the law, to redeem those under the law, that we might receive adoption to sonship. Because you are his sons, God sent the Spirit of his Son into our hearts, the Spirit who calls out, "Abba, Father." So you are no longer a slave, but God's child; and since you are his child, God has made you also an heir. —Galatians 4:4-7 NIV

Wow. Do you understand what that means? You. Me. Adopted. By the God of the universe. Free to call Him Daddy. We've been adopted by the One who owns "the cattle on a thousand hills" (Psalm 50:10). Some of you may have been adopted by your parents and know how special it is to be chosen. God didn't have to choose us, but He did. Unlike the homeless man, we can and want to reap the benefit of our inheritance—blessings and benefits from God's great storehouse of grace.

Only when we understand that God has chosen us and adopted us into His family will we inherit those blessings. That is why the gospel —the story of Jesus dying on the cross for our sins—is called "the Good News."

Maybe you are hearing about your adoption by God and the Good News of your inheritance for the first time. I know it can be a bit confusing to understand, so we'll unpack what the Good News means on the next few pages. Go ahead—turn the page and discover how you can claim your inheritance!

# The Bad News and the Good News

### by Vicki Courtney

How many of you have heard someone say, "As long as you're a good person, you'll go to heaven"? I'm pretty sure I said it myself before I became a Christian. Unfortunately, it's not true. Years ago I did a survey at an event for middle and high school girls and asked the question, "What does it take to go to heaven?" Many of the girls at the event were Christians, so I couldn't believe it when most of their answers related to good deeds and "being good."

The bottom line is that we will never be able to earn our way to heaven with good deeds. I remember an example that a speaker used at an event years ago that really helped me better understand what it means to be a Christian and what it takes to get to heaven and spend eternity (forever and ever) with God. He said to imagine there were three people who claimed they could jump across the Grand Canyon. (Remember, this isn't a true story, so use your imagination!) The first person is just an aver-age guy who had done a few practice jumps in his front yard by running and jumping as far as he could the day before the Grand Canyon jump. The second person is super athletic. She is on the track team at her high school and had even won the long jump competition at her last track meet. The third person is an Olympic gold medalist in the long jump who holds the title of the world's best long jumper. Who do you think has the best chance of making it: person #1, person #2, or person #3? Obviously, the third person has the best shot of making it across!

What do you think happens? The first guy takes off running to make the jump and gets about ten feet before he plunges into the canyon. The second person, the athlete, is more confident, knowing she is in good physical shape and has trained much harder than the first guy. She takes off running and makes it out about fourteen feet, then plunges into the canyon. The third guy is the most qualified as an Olympic long jump champion. If anyone is going to be able to jump the Grand Canyon, he would be the guy. With confidence, he takes off running and makes a record jump of thirty feet! And then—yeah, you guessed it—he plunges into the canyon.

So, here's the deal: The average width of the Grand Canyon is ten miles, which converts to about 52,800 feet across. It didn't matter how many hours the Olympic long jumper had trained or how many feet he could jump—in the end, he would come up about 52,770 feet short.

First, the bad news. It is the same way when it comes to earning our way to heaven by trying to do enough good deeds. Isaiah 64:6 says, "All of us have become like one who is unclean, and all our righteous acts are like filthy rags" (NIV). *Righteous* means "good." It doesn't matter how good we are because we will never be able to match the purity and goodness of God. God cannot be in the presence of any sin, so if you have sinned even once (and trust me, you have), you cannot be in His presence. That's the bad news.

Now, for the good news! Jesus Christ came to bridge the gap between sinful man and a Holy God. The Bible tells us that there is no forgiveness of sins without the shedding of blood (Hebrews 9:22). When Jesus died on the cross, the shedding of His blood became the

sacrifice for our sins. Those who believe in Jesus Christ (Christians) believe that He has paid the penalty for their sins, and they can stand righteous (pure and holy) before God. God does not see their sins because they are washed clean by the blood of Christ.

What about that time last week when you talked back to your mother when she told you to clean your room? Forgotten. God doesn't see it. Or that time a few years ago when you stole some candy out of your brother's Halloween bucket, then lied and said you didn't? Forgotten. God doesn't see it. Or that time when you went online without your parents' permission and came across a website that was bad? Forgotten. God doesn't see it. It doesn't matter how many sins you have done or what they were—God doesn't see any of them or hold them against you. Poof—they're gone. Like magic. Remember, God can't be in the presence of sin because He's holy and perfect, so He sent Jesus to be the sacrifice for our sins so we could reach God. Jesus is the only way. He is our only hope. Without Him, we cannot reach God.

I'm not making this up. This is what the Bible says:

"We are made right with God by placing our faith in Jesus Christ. And this is true for everyone who believes, no matter who we are. For everyone has sinned; we all fall short of God's glorious standard. Yet God, in his grace, freely makes us right in his sight. He did this through Christ Jesus when he freed us from the penalty for our sins. For God presented Jesus as the sacrifice for sin. People are made right with God when they believe that Jesus sacrificed his life, shedding his blood" (Romans 3:22–25 NLT).

While the Bible tells us to seek to please God and do good works, there is no way to do enough good works to reach God on our own. We need help to make it across the Grand Canyon of sin. It doesn't matter how "good" we are; we will always fall short. That's where Jesus comes in. He is the only one who can make the jump. When you put your trust and faith in Jesus (believe He is the Son of God and forgiver of your sins), He makes the jump for you!

When you become a Christian, you are basically agreeing that you need Jesus to help you make the jump, and you accept that He is the only one who can remove your sins. And that is not just good news, but the best news you will ever hear!

So, what do you say?

God is standing on the other side of the Grand Canyon waiting for your answer. Don't make the jump of faith without Jesus!

## What About You?

1. Have you received Jesus into your heart and given your life to Him?

2. If so, describe what your relationship with Christ means to you.

3. If you haven't made the decision to follow Jesus yet, what questions do you have that you could ask an adult? This is not a decision to rush into, so take your time—but start asking those questions as soon as you are ready!

# Getting to Know God

## by Rachel Prochnow

Picture your best friend. Think about all the time the two of you have spent together. Remember all the secrets you've shared and the laughter that has bonded you together. Think about the countless hours you have spent getting to know each other. Do you think you would have become best friends if you hadn't spent that time together? The only way to grow closer to another person is to spend real, quality time with them. The same goes for your relationship with the Lord. I want to share with you some great ideas for creating a deeper and closer relationship with your Father in heaven. These are steps that I take on a daily basis that keep me moving closer to the Lord.

## 1. Spend Time in Prayer

I have found that writing my prayers down is a much more effective way for me to talk with the Lord. This keeps my mind focused on my prayers and prevents me from getting distracted. If journaling is not your thing, that's okay. The important thing is to make sure you spend time in prayer every day. Set aside a certain amount of time to talk with God. Tell Him what you are struggling with, what is weighing on your heart, your hopes, and what you are feeling. Allow His Spirit to draw you closer to Him. First Thessalonians 5:17 tells us to "pray constantly." You don't have to have your eyes closed and your hands folded for prayer. Prayer is like having an ongoing conversation with God throughout the day.

## 2. Read Your Bible

One of the simplest things you can do to grow closer to the Lord is read your Bible. The Bible is our instruction manual for living. Set aside time to read the Word of God every day. Doing this will help you to understand the heart of God and know Him more intimately. Psalm 1:2–3 says, "But his delight is in the law of the LORD, and in His law he meditates day and night. He shall be like a tree planted by the rivers of water, that brings forth its fruit in its season, whose leaf shall not wither; and whatever he does shall prosper" (NKJV). Do you delight in the law of the Lord (the Bible)?

## 3. Find a Church

If you want to get to know God, it's important to be a part of a Bible-believing church where you are in the company of other believers. Attending church will reinforce your faith and keep it strong. I know you don't have much control over whether you attend church regularly since you are dependent on your parents to take you. If necessary, tell them why it's important to you to attend church every week. If they are unable to take you, see if you can find a friend who lives nearby and ask if they can give you a ride.

## 4. Choose Friends Who Love the Lord

You can tell a lot about a person by the friends they choose. Choose friends who love and respect God. Choose friends who will encourage you and challenge you to walk closer with the Lord.

First Corinthians 15:33 states, "Do not be deceived: 'Bad company corrupts good morals'" (NASB). The friends you choose matter.

## 5. Find a Mentor

Think about someone who is older who can help you in your walk with the Lord. Maybe it's your mom, or a teacher, or a youth leader at your church. These women have been through many of the same things you have, but they are a few steps ahead of you in the journey.

They have struggled with the same temptations. Choose someone who you know loves the Lord, who loves you, and who you know you can trust. Ask her to help you dig into the Word and to help you live the life worthy of the calling you have received.

Just like the time you spend with your best friend, you have to spend time with the Lord to get to know Him. You need to spend time in prayer and in His Word. It's also helpful to have others encouraging you to walk closer to Him through friendship. God wants us to be in a community of fellow believers, spurring each other closer to Him.

One of the things that sets Christianity apart from all other world religions is that our God (the one, true God) wants to have a personal relationship with us. Not a day should go by that we are not amazed by that fact. The best way to thank Him is to take Him up on the offer and get to know Him.

## What About You?

1. Are you growing closer to God right now or just kind of stumbling through your spiritual walk?

2. If you are struggling, what's keeping you from doing what it takes to grow closer to God?

3. Which of the helpful hints listed above do you think will be the hardest for you to do?

4. Which steps are you already taking? How are they helping your journey?

# Hello, God, Are You There?

Wouldn't it be awesome if there was someone we could go to when we had a question or needed help? Oh, wait a minute . . . THERE IS! Sometimes it is easy to forget that God is *always* listening. In fact, He *wants* to hear from you! How cool is that? In Luke 11:9, the Lord says, "So I say to you: Ask and it will be given to you; seek and you will find; knock and the door will be opened to you" (NIV). The Lord clearly tells us in this verse to come to Him, and He will answer us. However, keep in mind that God doesn't always give us the answers we want. Sometimes He doesn't answer a prayer the way we would like it to be answered, so we have to trust that He always knows what is best.

Read below and check out how God has answered the prayers of these girls who are just like you!

When we moved from Pennsylvania to Illinois, I prayed and asked God for friends. He gave me a friend who also had a younger sister like I do, and now our sisters are friends too! So He not only answered my prayer for a friend, but He gave my sister a friend too!

Kaitlin, 12

I prayed for my friend's mom for a long time because she had cancer. God healed her from her cancer, and now she's healthy.

Mallory, 9

When I took the STAAR test, I was really nervous. I did not want to get a bad grade. I asked God to help me stay calm and not freak out. He helped me stay focused through the whole test, and I got a good grade too.

Kylee, 9

One night my mom came to tuck me in and say my prayers, and she felt so sick. So when she left, I prayed with my prayer bear for God to help my mom feel better—and the next morning she was feeling better.

Lucy, 9

I have a medical problem that was very embarrassing for me. I prayed for a very long time for God to heal me. I trusted Him the whole time and believed that He would answer my prayer. And He did. I am much better now, and I keep getting better and better every week.

Emily, 9

I used to be scared to sleep over at friends' houses. I prayed that God would take my fear away. My mom and I made up a song to Isaiah 41:10, and I would sing it to help me fight my fear. God answered my prayers and helped me through my fearful time. Now I love sleepovers!

Amelia, 12

I prayed for my friendship with another girl I've known since we were four years old. We have been in elementary classes from the beginning. My friend started getting distant and cold. I told God that I loved my friend, I have known her for so long, and I wanted her friendship to be better. So I asked God to help me. I wrote her a letter telling her I wanted to be good friends. Now we are good friends again.

Lydia, 8

When we were flying to China to adopt my baby brother . . . I prayed for God to please let the plane land safely . . . and He did!

McKenna, 12

When I was ending third grade, I started praying to have a certain fourth-grade teacher. I prayed all through the summer, and then before school started, I found out I didn't get that teacher. At first I was disappointed, but after a while, I realized God had something better for me, and I loved the teacher I got. So He said no to my prayer, but He did that because He had something better and knew what was best for me.

Lucy, 11

My family was helping to renovate a trailer for another family. I prayed that it would be a success so the family would have a home, and God provided everyone and everything so this family would have a home to live in.

Brooke, 11

I prayed that my daddy would get a job here in Georgia, and God provided a job!

Lacey, 8

When my grandmother got breast cancer I prayed that God would heal her and make her stronger. I prayed that she would survive and live life to the fullest. My grandmother is now doing great.

Anslee, 11

I prayed about my test, and I could feel Him with me helping to keep me calm and focused.

Claire, 10

A few years ago my friend's little sister had cancer, and I prayed every day that God would heal her and make her free from her cancer. He answered my prayers. She doesn't have cancer anymore.

Natalie, 10

When my grandmother had surgery on her hand, I asked for God to help her through the surgery and have a good recovery.

Caroline, 10

I prayed that God would help me be friends with a new girl at our school who was having a hard time adjusting. Now we are good friends. Yay!

Bailey, 9

I prayed that the caterpillar that I was taking care of wouldn't die and would turn into a butterfly. It did turn into a butterfly!

Olivia, 11

I prayed, and God helped me to do good on a test, and I got an A+.

Mya, 10

I asked God to heal Roxy (my dog) when she was really hurt, and she's better now.

Noelle, 12

I prayed that God would allow us to buy a house, and He did.

Mollie Frances, 10

# Too Busy for God?

## by Whitney Prosperi

Have you ever noticed that it's cool to have a lot going on? I mean, when someone asks you what you've been doing, you don't want to say you've been sitting at home and staring out the window. You want to have something to say. Everyone in our culture seems to want to have lots going on. Many people like to stay busy because it makes them feel important or gives them purpose.

Whatever the case may be, if we're too busy for God, we're just too busy. Period. If you find yourself in this situation, read on. You'll discover some helpful ways to make time for God in spite of a busy day or a busy life.

## Make time with God a priority.

You've probably heard it said that we find time for what we really care about. You probably take the time to brush your hair and get ready each morning. Most likely you give some attention to responding to a party invitation or your favorite TV show. And you don't miss out on important conversations with your best friend. So why is it that time with God is often the last thing on our list? We do it if we find extra time, but when other things come up, it's usually the first thing to go.

Could it be that we know God will forgive us? I mean, that is His specialty, right? We can't always be assured our teacher will forgive us if we're late or that a friend will not hold it against us if we forget to call her back. So we take advantage of His forgiveness, knowing that He'll be waiting for us the next time.

But why not make time with God our top priority? That way, other things may not get done or other people may not hear back from us, but God will. We just determine that time with Him is the last thing we toss out on a busy day. If you're willing to make that commitment, stop right now and pray. Ask Him to help you commit to spending time with Him each day, whether it is first thing in the morning, right after school, or before bed.

## Say no to something else.

While it's not popular to say no to opportunities that come up, sometimes we just have to if we're going to make time with God a top priority. Maybe you're involved in something that takes so much of your time that you're unable to keep your commitment to spend time alone with God. It could be a particular extracurricular activity or interest. If this is the case, consider talking to your parents about cutting back on time spent on this activity. Or you might even want to take a break from it altogether. You can always get involved in that activity later. The world won't end. I promise. And you might even find that you enjoy having a little free time to explore other interests. Or maybe there is something else you can cut back on so you can spend more time with God. It could be time spent on the computer, watching TV, or playing games on your tablet. Saying no to something else will mean that you can say yes to the very best of all—Jesus.

You probably remember the story of the two sisters, Mary and Martha, in the Bible. Martha was very busy. She would have fit in beautifully in our culture. But Mary chose to spend time with Jesus. She knew what was most important. She remembered what would matter in the course of forever. Jesus corrected Martha for the way she misplaced priorities and praised Mary for her choices. Luke 10:41–42 says, "'Martha, Martha,' the Lord answered, 'you are worried and upset about many things, but few things are needed—or indeed only one. Mary has chosen what is better, and it will not be taken away from her'" (NIV).

Which sister do you identify with more: Mary or Martha? Will you choose the many things that really don't make a difference, or the one thing that is absolutely needed? Make the right choice, like Mary—and you won't regret it. Ever.

## Schedule time with God.

If you're going to spend time with God on a regular basis, you have got to set aside the time each day to do it. Make an appointment with God. It might be in the morning or the evening. It could be during lunch or right after school. What works best for you? For many, the morning is the best time to spend with God. Before the day begins with all of its distractions and temptations, you can focus on the words you read in your Bible and be encouraged by them.

Psalm 143:8 says, "Let me experience Your faithful love in the morning, for I trust in You. Reveal to me the way I should go because I long for You." What an awesome way to start the day—by asking God to show us the right path!

Do whatever it takes to find time in your day. The more time you spend with God, the more this will be an irreplaceable step to your day as well.

## Ask a friend for help.

Have you ever noticed that we have an easier time keeping our commitment when we know someone else has made the same one? I used to work out with a friend every morning at six. Now, you can bet I wouldn't have dragged myself out of bed if I didn't know she was waiting for me. Having someone who was committed to the same thing helped me keep my commitment to getting in shape.

It's the same way in our relationship with God. If you know you want to get up each morning for time alone with God but also know you have a hard time crawling out of bed in the morning, ask a friend to help you. Now, I don't mean that she comes to your house and kicks you out of bed. Just agree together to pray for one another. Check in and ask each other how it's going every now and then.

## Don't be hard on yourself.

If you miss one day, don't throw in the towel. Just pick up the next day where you left off. Or find a few minutes later in the day to touch base with God. He isn't going to be mad or punish you. He's not asking you to be perfect. He wants you to get to know Him. Remember that this is a relationship. He is waiting to hear from you. Isaiah 30:18 says, "Therefore the LORD is waiting to show you mercy, and is rising up to show you compassion, for the LORD is a just God. All who wait patiently for Him are happy."

## What About You?

1. Is spending time with God each day a priority in your life?

2. Is there an activity or a relationship that you need to step back from in order to have more time with God?

3. If so, how are you going to take the first steps in doing this?

# Dig into God's Word

## by Susan Palacio

Have you ever been to a museum and seen fossils? Maybe you've seen one of a dinosaur, insect, or fish. It always amazes me that scientists take months, and sometimes even years, to carefully dig through tons and tons of dirt just to find the skeleton of something that lived and died a very long time ago. But to them, excavating that skeleton was important, crucial even, to their jobs. They valued the information that the skeleton would give them and gladly did the work to get to their "treasure," the fossil.

Sometimes studying the Bible is the same way. To really get to the treasure, we must first do some digging. Reading and understanding the Bible isn't always easy, but the reward is well worth the work!

### THE TOOLS

Before we can begin digging, we need to understand the tools we'll be using.

### 1. Bible

*Layout:* The Bible is divided into two sections, the Old Testament and New Testament. The entire Bible is God's inspired work, so it is all-important, and it has the same message of redemption from beginning to end.

The Old Testament takes place from creation to a time prior to Jesus' birth. The Old and New Testaments have about a four-hundred-year gap between them. The New Testament picks up with Jesus being born. Revelation ends the New Testament with the prophecy, or future-telling, of the end of times here on earth as well as a glimpse of what we can expect afterward in heaven.

In the New Testament, if your Bible has red words, it means that Jesus said them.

*Table of Contents:* Sometimes it can be hard to find a particular book. So each Bible has a list in the first few pages to tell you the order, and even a starting page number, for each of the sixty-six books. From there, you'd look for the chapter and verse. When you see a passage listed like this, John 3:16, it is referencing the book of John, the third chapter, sixteenth verse.

## 2. Concordance

Most Bibles include a listing near the back where you can find verses that include a particular word. Let's say you wanted to look up a verse about being afraid. If you looked up the word *afraid*, you'd find Psalm 56:3, "When I am afraid, I will trust in You."

Most Bibles also include cross-references or footnotes. These are teeny little letters you sometimes see slightly above a word in a verse. It looks like this: [a]. If this appears over a word, it is telling you that either this word appears in other similar verses or it includes a note about that particular word or verse. The cross-references are usually listed in the middle column on the page or at the very bottom. You would look at the chapter and verse you were reading, then find the matching letter in the notes section. If it is a cross-reference, it will list other verses that include the referenced word. If it is a footnote (usually at the bottom of the page), it will tell you something about that word.

## 3. Journal

While a journal is not absolutely necessary, it can be a very helpful tool to write out the things that God teaches you.

## THE TREASURE MAP

So you've got the tools; now you need the map to the treasure! Below is a handy format to use when studying Scripture. Follow these steps and begin digging.

### See

First things first. Read it and let it sink in a little. Don't read too much at a time so you can focus. Look for words that are repeated, words that are strong or action-oriented, words that stand out, and words such as *therefore* and *so* (they indicate cause-and-effect relationships).

### Think

Think about what the verses are trying to communicate. Ask yourself these questions:

*What do these verses mean?*
*What is the theme?*
*Is it asking me to do something?*

Look for patterns that compare things, such as "the wise man does X, but the foolish man does Y," and make a chart with lists underneath each category.

If you have a hard time understanding what certain verses mean, do not be shy about asking Mom, Dad, or a church teacher about it. Another idea is to use a Bible written in a translation that is easier to understand.

## Feel

Ask yourself, *After reading and thinking about the meaning of these verses, how does it affect my feelings toward God, myself, and others? Does it reveal a sin that I should feel sorry about? Does it make me love God more because I have learned about him?* For example, reading John 3:16 might make you feel grateful to God for sending Jesus to save us.

## Do

Time for action! *How does this verse affect my behavior or thoughts? Does it show me how to think or act differently than I already do? How can I apply this verse to my life?*

## IT'S TIME TO DIG!

Reference the "treasure map" to help you excavate God's truth by looking at James 1:19–20. Write out some thoughts to these questions to help you.

1. See: *What words jump out to me?*

2. Think: *What do these verses mean?*

3. Feel: *How do these verses make me feel about God, myself, or others?*

4. Do: *What am I going to do in my life now because of these verses?*

Finish by praying. It's always important to pray while you are reading and studying the Bible. Ask God to show you the treasure that He wants you to have from reading His Word. Happy digging!

## Where to Dig

Here are some Bible reading plans to give you an idea of where to start digging into God's Word on a regular basis.

- *Proverb a day for a month*

  Read one chapter a day from Proverbs for one month. Since Proverbs has 31 chapters, you can read the entire book of Proverbs in one month.

- *Psalm a day for a year*

  Read one chapter a day from Psalms for the entire year and you will read through the book of Psalms twice.

- *Psalm and a proverb a day for five months*

  Read one chapter from the book of Psalms and one chapter from the book of Proverbs a day for five months, and you will read through the book of Psalms once and book of Proverbs five times.

- *Five verses a day*

  Read five verses a day from anywhere in the Bible.

- *Topical*

  Look up verses in your concordance about a particular topic, and study a different topic each week.

## FOR THE DEEP-DIGGERS

- *One New Testament chapter a day for a year.*

  Read one chapter a day from the New Testament five days a week. This will allow you to read through the entire New Testament in a year (260 chapters).

- *One New Testament book a month*

  Choose a shorter New Testament book to read every week (usually about one chapter a day) for the entire month. By the end of the month, you will have read through the book four times (which helps you remember it!).

  Some suggestions: January: James; February: Philippians; March: 1 John; April: 1 Peter; May: 2 Peter; June: 1 Timothy; July: Ephesians; August: Galatians; September: Colossians; October: 1 Thessalonians; November: Titus; December: 2 Timothy.

# The Heart of the Matter

## by Vicki Courtney

### Did you know?

- Your heart was the first organ to begin functioning when you were in your mother's womb.

- Your heart is the hardest-working muscle in your body.

- Your heart is approximately the same size as your fist.

- Your heart beats 100,000 times a day, 35 million times a year, and 2.5 billion times a lifetime (on average).

- In an average lifetime, the heart pumps one million barrels of blood.

- Enough power is generated in the heart in one day to drive a car twenty miles.

- The human heart can create enough pressure to squirt blood at a distance of thirty feet.

Okay, so I know that last fact was a bit gross, but c'mon, you have to admit—that's pretty cool! Obviously it's important to take care of your heart so you can live a long and healthy life. If someone doesn't take good care of their heart, they can get heart disease. Heart disease can lead to a heart attack, and a heart attack can lead to death. But the good news is that heart disease can be prevented. Doctors recommend two things: diet and exercise.

So, why am I telling you this? You're young, and it's not like you're at risk of heart disease, but believe it or not, you are at risk of another kind of heart attack—a spiritual heart attack. The Bible says to guard your heart. But what exactly does that mean? Basically it means to protect your heart from things that could cause damage and affect your relationship with God—the One who knit your heart together. And amazingly, the same two things that doctors recommend to help prevent a real-live heart attack are the same two things Christians can do to prevent a spiritual heart attack: diet and exercise.

## Diet

Have you ever heard that saying, "Garbage in, garbage out"? It basically means whatever you put into your heart will affect your actions. For example, if you only eat junk food and never eat healthy foods, your body will not be as healthy as it should be. And just as food can affect the physical condition of your heart, TV shows, music, movies, friends, and other influences can affect the spiritual condition of your heart.

I often tell teenage girls who really want a boyfriend that if they're not careful, it can cause spiritual damage to their hearts. If they get too focused on their boyfriend and he's all they think about, then they won't be as close in their relationship with God, right?

## Exercise

Just like it's important to exercise regularly to have a healthy heart, it's also important to exercise spiritually to have a healthy heart. Spiritual exercise includes prayer (talking to God just like you would a close friend) and reading your Bible. Sometimes it's hard for young people to read their Bibles regularly because they don't always understand what they are reading. That's why I write books like the one you are holding in your hands—so that you can read stories and examples that help you better understand Scripture as you read it.

So, what do you say? Is your heart in good shape? If not, it's not too late to change your diet (be careful what you watch, listen to, and who you hang out with) and start exercising (praying and reading your Bible)! And if you ask me, that's way better for you than doing a thousand-kadrillion jumping jacks in gym class. Just don't tell your PE teacher I said that!

# Guard Your Heart

1. Just for fun, draw a picture of a "guarded heart."

   *(Hint: Think of a fence that guards a garden or backyard.)*

2. Can you think of a TV show, movie, or song that you saw or heard where you were left feeling uncomfortable, like it wasn't good for your heart?

3. How might you change your daily diet to have a healthier heart (spiritually)?

4. What are some ways you are exercising your heart (spiritually)?

   *(Hint: Read your Bible, pray, or go to church.)*

5. How might you need to improve your daily "workout" plan to keep your heart in good shape?

Take a minute to talk to God and ask Him to help you guard your heart. What's cool is that even as you are praying and asking Him to help you, you are exercising your heart at that very moment!

# Who's Your Hero?

## by Vicki Courtney

Everybody has a hero. I'm pretty sure my first hero was my dad. Maybe it was because there's a picture of him holding me up proudly at a New Year's Eve party for all his friends to see. I was only six weeks old at the time. My mother claims he stole me out of my crib minutes before midnight and proudly danced around the living room with me in his arms. I loved looking at that picture.

Or maybe he earned hero status when I lost the grocery store coloring contest at the age of four. I tried so hard to stay in the lines and was sure that my efforts would earn me the grand prize. When my younger brother and I saw someone else's picture posted on the bulletin board the next time we were in the grocery store, my dad ushered us to the car and drove us straight to the drugstore without saying a word. Minutes later, he came out of the store with a bag, opened the car door, and pulled out two brightly colored radios (a lot like you getting a new iPod today). Only a hero would do something like that. In the years that followed, he would often refer to me as his "little valentine," and he even made up a song about my ponytails. He sang it every time I wore ponytails, so I made sure to wear them a lot.

My friends always said I was a "daddy's girl" and "spoiled." Maybe it was because I got a brand-new, fire-engine red Ford Mustang my freshman year in college. When I would come home on an occasional weekend in college, my dad would follow me out to my car and slip money into my hand when he hugged me in the driveway.

My dad was the one I called when I failed one of my college classes. I knew he wouldn't blow up and would calmly tell me, "Just try harder next time." When I was newly married and my grandfather was dying, my dad would fly into Austin so we could make the two-hour drive together to spend time with my grandfather in Houston. One time, I accidentally left my purse at a restaurant along the way and realized it about thirty miles later. When I told my dad, he said, "No problem, honey. Things like that happen," and promptly turned the car around and headed back to get it.

As I've gotten older, I've gained a

better understanding of why every little girl wants a hero. God wired our hearts that way in the hopes that we would seek Him. We long to be adored and to adore in return. Most of all, we want to be rescued. That's why we're drawn to the hero in every love story. You know, the one who sweeps in and rescues the princess from some sort of miserable situation. A villain. An evil stepmother. The endless job of sweeping out chimneys. When it comes to rescue missions, what Jesus did tops them all. Since God can't be in the presence of sin because He is holy and pure, Jesus bridged the gap so we could spend eternity (life after we die) with God. He stepped in and offered to pay the penalty for our sins even though He had never sinned Himself.

One of my favorite verses in the Bible is Romans 5:8. It says, "But God proves His own love for us in that while we were still sinners, Christ died for us!" Think about that one word, *still*. If you look it up in the dictionary, you would find this definition: "in the future as in the past."

Now read the verse again with the meaning inserted: "But God proves His own love for us in that while we were [in the future as in the past] sinners, Christ died for us!" Christ died for us even though He knew we would continue to sin . . . in the future, just as we had sinned in the past. How amazing is that? It sounds pretty heroic to me.

Who is your hero?

## What About You?

1. If you had to name a hero (other than Jesus), who would it be? Why?

2. Why do you think we want a hero?

3. How did Jesus rescue us?

4. Is Jesus your one, true Hero?

Other than Jesus, who is your hero, and why?

Scan for Video Answers!

191

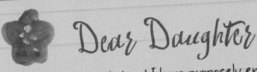

# Dear Daughter

Since you were a little girl, your dad and I have purposely encouraged you in lots of areas. We've told you how smart you are (and you amaze me sometimes!). We've told you that you are pretty—and you are (we are already worried about the dating years). We've praised you for working hard and keeping at it when learning something new. And we've tried to encourage you to like yourself.

When we say those things, though, we both feel like we are walking a tightrope. We want you to feel good about yourself, but we don't want you to think your worth is based on the good character traits and skills we see in you. We want you to be confident, but not self-centered. We want you to be humble, but still be okay with who you are.

Your dad and I want you to believe one very important truth: Your worth doesn't come from what you do, what you look like, or what other people think about you. Your worth comes from one place: God. I know that may sound kind of lame, but it's true.

We've read the Bible to you and tried to talk about what it says about your worth:

For it was You who created my inward parts;
You knit me together in my mother's womb.
I will praise You

because I have been remarkably and wonderfully made.
Your works are wonderful,
and I know this very well.—Psalm 139:13–14

Aren't five sparrows sold for two pennies? Yet not one of them is forgotten in God's sight. Indeed, the hairs of your head are all counted. Don't be afraid; you are worth more than many sparrows!—Luke 12:6–7

Why am I telling you this? Because you are about to enter a time in your life when other voices are going to become much louder than ours. You may already be hearing them now. Bullies who call you fat or coaches who don't believe in you. Boys who want you to act a certain way. It's all yelling at you, trying to tell you who you are and what makes you important.

I want you to remember one thing: only the One who made you has the right to label you.

Ever since you were a little girl, you've hated labels in your clothes. You tear them out of your shirts as soon as you get home. The labels in your pants may last a little longer, but eventually they get ripped out too. They are itchy and uncomfortable and irritating. They've got to go!

Have you ever thought about why those labels are there? It's not just so I can know whether or not to dry your shirt! Labels indicate the manufacturer. Who made that shirt? Or those pants? Sometimes labels come in handy when we want to buy more of that same item because it's wearing out—like your favorite blue shirt you've worn all summer long. And the only person who gets to put that label on any item is the company that made it. Walmart wouldn't allow Target to put its tags in Walmart's clothes, right?

Again: The only one who has the right to label you is the One who made you.

God Almighty. The One who flung a million galaxies into space and names every star (Psalm 147:4) also formed every swirl in your fingerprints and every freckle on your face. The One who split the Red Sea in half for the Israelites gave your hair that natural part. He is your manufacturer, so to speak. And He's the only one with the right to tell you who you are.

And if God has called you beautiful, delightful, and dearly loved (and He calls you all of those things in Scripture), then why would you let other people put a different label on you?

Just like those labels you hate on clothes, I hope you will refuse to wear the labels that others try to put on you. I hope you rip them off. I pray that you choose to believe what God says about you, because what God says is always true.

God calls you precious in His sight and honored and loved (Isaiah 43:4).

He ought to know. He made you.

Why would you believe anyone else?

Love,
Mom

# God Values Wisdom

## by Vicki Courtney

*My child, if your heart is wise, my own heart will rejoice! Everything in me will celebrate when you speak what is right. Don't envy sinners, but always continue to fear the LORD. You will be rewarded for this; your hope will not be disappointed. My child, listen and be wise: Keep your heart on the right course.* —Proverbs 23:15–19 NLT

There is a story told about four people flying in a small, four-passenger plane: a pilot, a minister, and two teenagers, one of whom had just won an award for being the Smartest Teenager in the World.

As they were flying along, the pilot turned to the three passengers and said, "I've got some bad news, and I've got some worse news. The bad news is, we're out of gas. The plane's going down, and we're gonna crash. The worse news is, I only have three parachutes on board."

This meant, of course, that someone would have to go down with the plane. The pilot continued, "I have a wife and three children at home. I have many responsibilities. I'm sorry, but I'm going to have to take one of the parachutes." With that, he grabbed one of the chutes and jumped out of the plane.

The Smartest Teenager in the World was next to speak. "I'm the Smartest Teenager in the World," he said. "I might be the one who comes up with a cure for cancer or solves the world's economic problems. Everyone is counting on me!" The Smartest Teenager in the World grabbed the second parachute and jumped.

The minister then spoke up and said, "Son, you take the last parachute. I've made my peace with God, and I'm willing to go down with the plane. Take the last parachute and go."

"Relax, Reverend," said the other teenager. "The Smartest Teenager in the World just jumped out of the plane with my backpack."

Of course the story is not true, but it was meant to make a point. As you grow up, you'll meet many smart people. Maybe you're one of them! However, being smart doesn't always make you wise. Proverbs 23:15 reminds us that God will rejoice if you become wise.

Did you catch that? It didn't say, "I will rejoice if you make straight A's" or "I will rejoice if you make the Honor Roll."

Now take a look at verse 16. Does it say, "Everything in me will celebrate when you make a 100 on the spelling test"? Or does it say, "My heart will thrill when your project wins a ribbon in the science fair"? No! It says, "Everything in me will celebrate when you speak what is right" (NLT).

Being smart may earn you good grades, academic awards, college scholarships, and possibly a good job someday. But being smart doesn't guarantee you a happy future. If you want a future and a hope, listen and be wise. Keep your heart on the right course. You don't want to be the one grabbing the backpack. Go for the parachute!

## What About You?

1. Can you think of someone you know (don't mention names) who is smart and makes good grades, but he or she doesn't have much common sense or wisdom?

2. What do you think is more important in our world today: being smart or being wise? Why?

3. Have you ever been to an awards ceremony where someone was rewarded for having wisdom and making good choices?

4. If God hands out awards in heaven, what do you think would be more important to Him: intelligence or wisdom?

# Treasures in Heaven

## by Vicki Courtney

*I* once heard someone say, "You never see a U-Haul behind a hearse." When we look around at all our possessions, it's easy to forget that we are born into this world with nothing and we will leave this world with nothing. I was reminded of this truth when my grandparents passed away. They were not wealthy, but they lived a comfortable life. Yet in the end, their home, cars, jewels, and other treasured possessions were left behind for their children and grandchildren to go through and decide what to keep and what to sell. I have a few of their treasured possessions, such as my grandmother's Bible, my grandfather's watch, their old love letters from when they were dating, and even a Christmas ornament that used to hang on their tree each year. My grandparents' possessions have been divided up among family members, but it's the memories we cling to rather than the treasures.

When they passed away, it got me thinking about the day we show up at the gates of heaven, mere souls with nothing to show from our earthly stay. No tablets or smartphones in hand. No trophies that lined our bookshelves in our childhood bedrooms or certificates proving our perfect attendance in third grade. No report cards or paychecks. No money or credit cards. No closets full of clothes and shoes. Everything you own will be left behind. While that sounds pretty depressing, you don't have to show up empty-handed!

In the sixth chapter of Matthew, Jesus shared the secret to having treasures in heaven. He said:

*"Don't collect for yourselves treasures on earth, where moth and rust destroy and where thieves break in and steal. But collect for yourselves treasures in heaven, where neither moth nor rust destroys, and where thieves don't break in and steal. For where your treasure is, there your heart will be also." (Matthew 6:19–21)*

This doesn't mean that it's wrong to have nice things. The point Jesus was trying to make was that our "earthly treasures" shouldn't be more important than our "heavenly treasures." Sadly, most people in the world (including many Christians) will spend the majority of their time and money storing up treasures on earth rather than storing up treasures in heaven. Don't be fooled. You're not too young to begin storing up treasures in heaven.

Maybe you're not sure what would be considered a "heavenly treasure." Take a look at the list below to help you better understand the difference.

## Earthly Treasures

Your very own tablet or smartphone.

Those little figurines you collect that sit on a shelf.

Your favorite blankie from when you were a baby—the one your dad drove thirty miles to go back and get after you left it behind at a restaurant on a family vacation.

The gift cards you got for Christmas. All of your Christmas gifts. And birthday gifts. Every year. For the rest of your life.

That killer new pair of Converses you finally talked your mom into buying for you.

The stack of certificates you received at the end of the school year for being an awesome student.

The ribbon you got for winning the science fair.

Your family. (Yes, this includes your pesky younger brother.)

Your best friend.

Your pet cat, Lulu-Belle.

The bazillion songs on your iPod.

## Heavenly Treasures

That time you sat by the new girl at lunch when you saw her sitting alone.

The wildflowers you picked for your grandmother and gave to her for no reason at all.

When you refused to gossip with a friend about one of your other friends.

That time you volunteered to walk your neighbor's dog when she sprained her ankle.

When you shared about Jesus at a sleepover with your friends and told them about God's love.

The mission trip you went on, when you led a vacation Bible school for kids who are less fortunate.

The canned-food drive you organized in your neighborhood to help needy families over the holidays.

Each and every one of your prayers for friends and family members who don't know Jesus.

The Bible you bought for your friend when she mentioned she didn't have one.

When you do something wrong and you confess it to God and ask for forgiveness.

When you praise God.

Let me make it clear that it's not wrong to love your possessions. In fact, it's perfectly normal. The problem comes when your affection for earthly treasures is greater than your affection for heavenly treasures. If you had to think long and hard about the heavenly treasures you are storing up, chances are, you are more focused on earthly treasures.

Do you want to show up empty-handed when you exit this world? Now is the time to think about the treasures you are storing up in heaven. If you love God and are grateful for His gift of grace, your life will show it. You can't help but have treasures in heaven because you will want others to have that same gift. Moths and rust can't touch it. Thieves can't steal it. It's yours—from here to eternity.

# What About You?

1. Do you think about heavenly treasures very often?

2. What is an example of a treasure you are storing in heaven (something you have done that was pleasing to God)?

3. Why do you think it's easier to focus on earthly treasures than heavenly treasures?

4. What can you do differently to shift your attention from the things of this world to actions and attitudes that please God?

# Think This, Not That

## by Tami Overhauser

When lies creep in and create doubt about your faith or about Jesus, use the Word of God as your weapon. Replace those lies with these truths.

> You will know the truth, and the truth will set you free.—John 8:32

> Jesus told him, "I am the way, the truth, and the life. No one comes to the Father except through Me."—John 14:6

> The LORD is near to all who call on him, to all who call on him in truth.—Psalm 145:18 NIV

Give thanks to the Lᴏʀᴅ, for He is good;
His faithful love endures forever.—Psalm 107:1

For you are saved by grace through faith,
and this is not from yourselves;
it is God's gift.—Ephesians 2:8

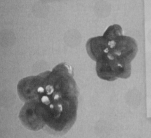

For everyone who calls on the name of the Lord
will be saved.—Romans 10:13

Therefore, if anyone is in Christ, he is a new creation;
old things have passed away, and look, new things have come.
—2 Corinthians 5:17

Do not fear, for I am with you; do not anxiously look about you, for I am your God. I will strengthen you, surely I will help you, surely I will uphold you with My righteous right hand.—Isaiah 41:10 NASB

Be strong and courageous. Do not be afraid or terrified because of them, for the Lᴏʀᴅ your God goes with you; he will never leave you nor forsake you. —Deuteronomy 31:6 NIV

For I will forgive their wickedness and will remember their sins no more.—Hebrews 8:12 NIV

For I am convinced that neither death nor life, neither angels nor demons, neither the present nor the future, nor any powers, neither height nor depth, nor anything else in all creation, will be able to separate us from the love of God that is in Christ Jesus our Lord.—Romans 8:38-39 NIV

# Are You A Christian?

## by Vicki Courtney

Wow, you made it to the end of the book! Congratulations! I realize some of you reading this book may not be quite sure of what it means to be a Christian. And others of you may have been told (by a parent, relative, or someone at your church) that you are a Christian, but you're still not really sure what that means. The truth is, no one can make that decision for you. You must make it for yourself. It is between you and God.

If you are not absolutely 100 percent sure that you are a Christian, please carefully read below what it means to be a follower of Christ. Remember, this is the most important decision you will ever make in your life. Read slowly and concentrate carefully on what the Bible verses mean. Don't worry, we'll take it slow and go step by step.*

---

\* Adapted from "Your Christian Life," written by the Billy Graham Evangelistic Association.

## We Learn About God's Love in the Bible

*"For God so loved the world that he gave his one and only Son, that whoever believes in him shall not perish but have eternal life" (John 3:16 NIV).*

God loves you. He wants to bless your life and make it full and complete. He wants to give you a life that will last forever, even after you die. *Perish* means to die and to be apart from God—forever. God wants you to have eternal life in heaven where you are with Him for eternity.

## We Are Sinful

*"For everyone has sinned; we all fall short of God's glorious standard" (Romans 3:23 NLT).*

You may have heard someone say, "I'm only human—nobody's perfect." This Bible verse says the same thing: we are all sinners. No one is perfect. When we sin, we do things that are wrong—things that God would not agree with. The verse says we fall short of "God's glorious standard."

Imagine that God gives you a test. Imagine that you have to make a 100 to meet God's "standard." It makes sense that you have to make a 100 because that's a perfect score, and God is perfect. Now let's say that everyone starts with a 100, but any time you sin (do something wrong), you get a point taken off. Since God is perfect and we are not, it is impossible for anyone to make a 100 on this test! I know it sounds like a strict rule, but think about it. If He is holy and perfect, He can't be around people who are not holy and perfect. If He allows sin into His presence, He won't be holy and perfect anymore. But before you start to worry that you don't meet His standard (you won't make a 100), just wait—there's good news ahead.

## Sin Has a Penalty (Punishment)

*"For the wages [cost] of sin is death"*
*(Romans 6:23 NIV).*

Just as criminals must pay the penalty for their crimes, sinners must pay the penalty for their sins. Imagine this: What if every time we did something wrong, we got a ticket (kind of like if you are driving too fast and you get a ticket as a punishment). Let's also say that our punishment is not that we have to pay money for our sins, but instead, we have to die. When we die, we will be separated from God for all eternity unless there is a way to pay

for our sins. The Bible teaches that those who choose to be separated from God will spend eternity in a place called hell. You may have heard some bad things about hell, but the worst part about hell is that you are in a place where you never receive any of God's blessings, only His eternal punishment.

## Christ Has Paid the Price for Our Sins!

*"But God proves His own love for us in that while we were still sinners, Christ died for us!" (Romans 5:8).*

The Bible teaches that Jesus Christ, the sinless (perfect) Son of God, has paid the price for all your sins. You may think you have to lead a good life and do good deeds before God will love you. It's good to do good deeds, but it won't pay the price for

## Christ Is at Your Heart's Door.

*"Here I am! I stand at the door and knock. If anyone hears my voice and opens the door, I will come in and eat with that person, and they with me"* (Revelation 3:20 NIV).

your sins and get you into heaven. No matter how many good deeds you do, you still won't get a 100 (a perfect score) on life's test. But the Bible says that Christ loved you enough to die for you, even when you were acting unlovable. Pretty amazing, huh?!

Jesus Christ wants to have a personal relationship with you. He wants to be your very best friend. He wants you to talk to Him just like you would talk to your best friend. Picture, if you will, Jesus Christ standing at the door of your heart and knocking. Invite Him in; He is waiting for you to receive Him into your heart as Lord and Savior.

## Salvation (Eternity in Heaven) Is a Free Gift.

*"God saved you by his grace when you believed. And you can't take credit for this; it is a gift from God. Salvation is not a reward for the good things we have done, so none of us can boast about it"* (Ephesians 2:8–9 NLT).

## You Must Receive Him.

*"But to all who did receive Him, He gave them the right to be children of God"* (John 1:12).

The word *grace* means a gift we don't deserve. It means Christ is offering to pay for something you could never pay for yourself: forgiveness of sins and eternal life. God's gift to you is free. You do not have to work for a gift—that's why it's called a gift. All you have to do is joyfully receive it. Believe with all your heart that Jesus Christ died for you and paid the price for your sins!

When you receive Christ into your heart you become a child of God, and you can talk to Him in prayer at any time about anything. The Christian life is a personal relationship with God through Jesus Christ. It's a relationship like the one you have with your parents and best friends. And best of all, it is a relationship that will last forever and ever. There is nothing you could ever do to make God stop loving you. Even though we will continue to sin, God still loves us. He never takes His gift back, so we don't have to worry about losing it. It is ours to keep forever.

So, what do you think about God's offer of forgiveness? Is this a gift you want to accept? If so, tell God. You don't have to say a fancy prayer—just talk to Him and tell Him that you believe that Jesus died on the cross for your sins and you want to receive that gift. That's all it takes! What are you waiting for? Stop and say a prayer right now.

Did you say a prayer and receive God's gift of forgiveness?

Sometimes people say a quick little prayer but never change the course of their lives. They continue along the same path and bank on that little prayer as a free ticket into heaven. No, we won't be perfect. Even though Christ has paid the penalty for our sins, we will still mess up. However, if you are a Christian, your life should show some proof of a changed heart. In the end, only you know if your decision to follow Christ is an honest decision.

If you did not understand some of the verses above and you still aren't quite sure where you stand when it comes to God's gift of eternal life, please talk to someone who can help you better understand what it means to be a Christian. Maybe it's your parents, pastor, youth minister, mentor, or a relative. Maybe it's a friend's mom. Find someone who knows what it means to be a Christian and tell them you want to know more. This is the most important truth you will ever know.

Whether you made the decision to become a Christian or not, it is my prayer that you have a better understanding of how much God loves you after reading this book. Never doubt your worth to Him. And when you do, stop and remember the cross.

# This is my prayer for you as you go forth and live out what you've learned:

I pray that out of his glorious riches he may strengthen you with power through his Spirit in your inner being, so that Christ may dwell in your hearts through faith. And I pray that you, being rooted and established in love, may have power, together with all the Lord's holy people, to grasp how wide and long and high and deep is the love of Christ, and to know this love that surpasses knowledge—that you may be filled to the measure of all the fullness of God.—Ephesians 3:16–19 NIV